Skip·Beat!

Skip·Beat!

1

Story & Art by Yoshiki Nakamura

Skip·Beat!

Volume 1

CONTENTS

SKIP BEAT 1

To readers I haven't seen a while, and to first-time readers, hello! I'm Nakamura. Whether you're browsing this at the bookstore, or sitting down and reading it thoroughly, thank you for reading my new series, *Skip Beat!* I would like to give this series a different story and character from my previous series, Kurepara (Tokyo Crazy Paradise). The way I want to develop the story is still a "secret." But because of that, readers who liked Kurepara might not like this so much... Starting with the main character—she's not a "hero of justice"...nor a "heroine" nor a "soothing heroine."

↑

I think this is a condition that must be present as the main characteristic of shojo manga...But I felt that type is an ordinary girl...and even if I don't do it, somebody else would draw it. The main character I draw must be a little like a wild beast, or even if I draw a traditional shojo manga main character, the readers won't enjoy it...I'm always obsessed by thoughts like that somewhere in my heart... (But that results in the tragedy of creating main characters that don't appeal to the general public)☺

...But regarding Kyoko's character, it was completed a long time ago, actually. Yes, when I was young, 19-21 years old...

Continued on page 8.

Act 1: And the Box Was Opened

Skip·

At my first job, a very depressing Kyoko character was created, who reflected my gray life (she could see spirits, and was good at witchcraft and making straw dolls for cursing people, so she was always a vengeful-spirit Kyoko). But although she could curse people, the curses usually failed. A silly character... Then I quit my first job and before I went to my second job, Kyoko's appearance changed a little (the changed Kyoko is on page 88), and after I made my debut as a mangaka, I drew a 30-page storyboard for a one-shot story with that Kyoko appearing as a side character.

↑ The antagonist's younger sister, an extremely evil personality.

...But before I could show it to my editor, I found out that my debut work would be a series. So I didn't show it to anybody, and it was put to sleep. But because I didn't use it then, I think I was able to use it now...Well, she has been changed for the series to be a little more cheerful than before. But the dark side is part of Kyoko's individuality, so she always has to be dark here and there. Because I have the image of the original Kyoko inside me, I have to be careful about showing the amount of darkness... It has to be in the range that is acceptable for a shojo manga heroine. By the way, when I was asked by my editor about ideas for the new series, I had in mind a simple school-based story... The main character was a bdautiful, angel-like girl hiding Kyoko inside...so there was a wide gap between her looks and her real personality, a character with poison. But, at that time I was doing a school-based story in *Hana to Yume*...

Continued on page 25.

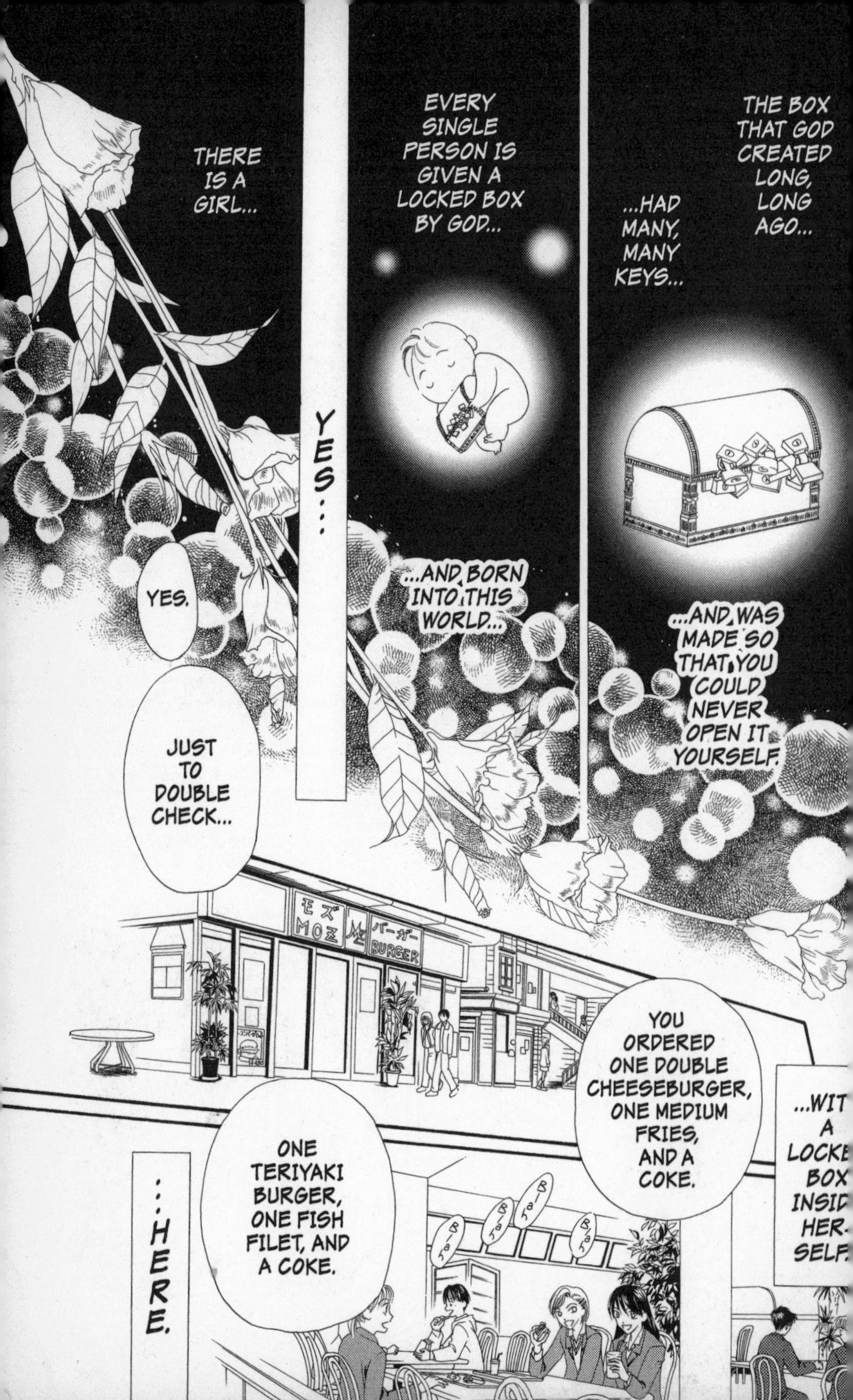

THE BOX THAT GOD CREATED LONG, LONG AGO...
...HAD MANY, MANY KEYS...
...AND WAS MADE SO THAT YOU COULD NEVER OPEN IT YOURSELF.
EVERY SINGLE PERSON IS GIVEN A LOCKED BOX BY GOD...
...AND BORN INTO THIS WORLD...
YES...
THERE IS A GIRL...
YES.
JUST TO DOUBLE CHECK...
モズ MOZ バーガー BURGER
...WIT A LOCKE BOX INSID HER-SELF.
YOU ORDERED ONE DOUBLE CHEESEBURGER, ONE MEDIUM FRIES, AND A COKE.
Blah
Blah
Blah
Blah
ONE TERIYAKI BURGER, ONE FISH FILET, AND A COKE.
...HERE.

IS THAT EVERY-THING?
...IVING OBLY...
MS. MOGAMI...
SORRY I'M LATE.
YOUR SHIFT IS OVER, I'LL SWITCH WITH YOU.
OH...
...YES.
SEE YOU LATER!
GOOD-BYE.
IT'S 5:10!
Oh, no!
CLOMP CLOMP
CLOMP CLOMP
Ahhhh!
I'VE GOT TO HURRY, OR I WON'T MAKE IT TO DARUMAYA BY 6!
Her next job.
She takes her clothes off as she runs.

Dressing Room
SHWA
SOOOO, IT'S SHO FROM NOW ON!!
TH-THUMP
SHO ...?
YOU MEAN SHO FUWA, THAT NEW POP STAR?
I SWITCHED TO SHO.
!!
YEAH!!
BECAUSE SHO SINGS BETTER, AND HE'S CUTE!
SHUP
Yeah, yeah.
Uh-huh.
Nya ha ha!
She's boasting.
....
HUH?
CHAK
HEY!
Wait a minute.
KUNIKO, WEREN'T YOU A REAL REN FAN?
ERK
HEY! DON'T TALK AS IF REN CAN'T SING AS WELL AS SHO!
I haven't actually heard him sing yet.
HE'S JUST AN ACTOR WHO LOOKS GOOD. OF COURSE HE CAN'T SING.
THE PROOF IS...
ANYWAY, I'M A SHO FAN NOW.

...THIS !!
Oh ho ho ho!
FWASH
SHO FU
I GOT TWO LIFE-SIZE POSTERS OF SHO FUWA WITH THE FIRST RELEASE OF HIS SECOND SINGLE!
?!
You mean you bought two of the same CD?
Ho Ho Ho!
One's for my collection.
Of course!
Seriously, she's serious.

IT... CAN'T BE...
I...
Th-thump
Th-thump
Th-thump
...BOUGHT TWO CDS, TOO...
A life-size poster?
With the first release?
What the HECK!!
...BUT I DIDN'T GET ANY POSTERS.
WH-
WHHYYYY!
My CD storeeeeee, Lalala!
200 miles down in the deep sea of despair.
Misery
HOW MEEEAAAN!
...
...
...
Deep-sea fish.

I WAITED ALL NIGHT FOR THE STORE TO OPEN BEFORE IT WENT ON SALE, AND BOUGHT IT RIGHT AWAY!
YOU DO THAT?
Normally?
......
It's not like it's a video game that everyone wants...
YOU DON'T HAVE TO LINE UP ALL NIGHT TO BUY IT.
staring
.....
SHO'S POSTERRRRRRR!
I want one tooOooo!
BYAAAA
A HAND FROM HER THROAT!!
EEEK!
fwap fwap
No, this is mine!
SCHLUUP
dizzy
ANGUISH
blub blub blub
Oh, no... She's sinking even deeper...
......
If we leave her like that, she's gonna suffocate.

HEY, MS. MOGAMI.
WHEN YOU BOUGHT THE CD, DIDN'T YOU GET A RECEIPT?
YES.
THEN SHOW THAT RECEIPT TO THE CASHIER ...
...AND ASK FOR A POSTER.
THEY MIGHT GIVE YOU AT LEAST ONE.
A ray of light ...
...in the deep sea ...
blub
blub
blub
THAT'S NOT GOING TO HAPPEN.
The store might argue.
A QUIET GIRL LIKE MS. MOGAMI CAN'T BE CONFRONTATIONAL LIKE THAT...
CRASH
DASH
BOMP
VUUU
BANG
BOMP
DASH
roll
roll
roll
....
I... ASSUMED THAT MS. MOGAMI WAS THE GENTLE, QUIET TYPE.
She works hard, never refuses requests ...
SHE RAN OFF...
At the speed of light...
AND...
I'm surprised...

...SHE SEEMED LIKE SHE HAD NO INTEREST IN CELEBRITIES WHATSO-EVER...

SO, MS. MOGAMI ...

...IS REALLY THE TYPE TO GET EXCITED ABOUT THESE THINGS...

THONK-A THONK-A THONK-A

AHH!

Huh?

SCREEEE

VOOM

Get out of my waaaa-aaaaay!

Eeek!

WHAT'S GOING ON?!

Ahh!

SHO'S POSTER!
THUMP
SCREEEEE
Plonk
Plonk
Plonk
Plonk
WHEEZE
WHEEZE
WHEEZE
WHEEZE
WHEEZE
I—
WHEEZE
I—
WHEEZE

... HAVEN'T RECEIVED ...
WHEEZE
WHEEZE
SHUP
WHEEZE
PANT
WHEEZE
PANT
... SHO'S ...
... POSTER ...
Now on Sale
New Album
Yammer Yammer
Wahhhh!
M- Manager!!
Ah-h h h h...
We're sorry. When you bought the CD, I hadn't told the staff members about the first release extras...
Um... we only have the store copy left...
Nervous
Scared
If you want this poster...
SHWUP

....
AH!
Happy...
I'M SO GLAD ...
..THAT THE STAFF MEMBERS WERE REASONABLE PEOPLE.
I DIDN'T HAVE PROOF THAT I HADN'T RECEIVED THE POSTERS, SO I ASSUMED THEY'D TELL ME THEY'D ALREADY GIVEN THEM TO ME.
THEY EVEN SAID THEY'D TRY TO GET ME ANOTHER ONE, IF THERE'RE ANY LEFT.
How nice! I'm Glad I was Brave enough to come! ♡
skrsh
NOW I CAN GO TO MY NEXT JOB—
skrsh skrsh
What ?!
?!
AAAHHHHHH!! NOOOOOO!
It's 5:45! The Taisho will scold me!

YOU DON'T HAVE TO MAKE IT IN 15!
HOW DID YOU MANAGE TO GET HERE SO FAST ?!
This Girl!
She was really reckless.
I...I'M ZHO... ZHORRY.
WHEEZE WHEEZE
Uhhhh
Gaaaaa
Ohhhhhh
Ehhhhhh
HERE, CAN YOU DRINK SOME WATER?
DRIBBLE
OH DEAR.
↑ She doesn't even have the strength to keep her mouth closed.
WELL, YOU WON'T BE ABLE TO WORK TONIGHT.
KA-CHAK
UM ...
... KYOKO ?
FWSSH
SHUFF
Huff Huff
Shedding her skin.

....
Shiver
shake
I... WHILL ... WHORK.
I BOUGHT SHO'S CD THIS MONTH...
...LIVING IN A REALLY EXPEN-SIVE APART-MENT?
You said you were working at another place, too.
....
WELL...
...IT'S ALL RIGHT...
If you don't want to talk about it.
IF I...
...EVEN TAKE A DAY OFF...
...I CAN'T...
...PAY MY RENT.
...
ARE YOU...
ARE YOU LIVING ALONE?
KYOKO...
...I DON'T KNOW WHAT'S GOING ON WITH YOU, BUT...
Th-thump
...COMING TO TOKYO RIGHT AFTER YOU GRADUATED FROM JUNIOR HIGH...
...AND WORKING ALL DAY, NOT EVEN GOING TO SENIOR HIGH... THERE'S SOMETHING WRONG.
.....
fwip fwip
ss shp
......

A YOUNG GIRL...
...WORKING HER TAIL OFF EVERYDAY...
You look even worse today.
But you always look pretty bad when you get here.
....
DON'T...
...YOU WANT TO...
...DRESS UP...
...LIKE OTHER GIRLS YOUR AGE?

KYOKO, YOU'RE ALWAYS ...

...READING STORIES ABOUT PRINCESSES.

EVEN IF SHE'S WEARING TATTERED CLOTHES, AND IS UNHAPPY...

...IN THE END SHE BECOMES MORE BEAUTIFUL THAN ANYBODY...

...AND IS LOVED BY EVERY-ONE...

...AND LIVES HAPPILY WITH THE PRINCE.

I LOVED STORIES ABOUT PRINCESSES LIKE THAT.

SOME-DAY...

...I WANT TO BE LIKE A PRINCESS TOO...

THAT...

...WAS MY CHILDHOOD DREAM.

BUT...

...AS I GREW UP, I REALIZED THAT IT TAKES MONEY TO BECOME BEAUTIFUL.

KA-TUNK KA-TUNK

DON'T YOU WANT TO DRESS UP?
gimme
gimme
gimme
gimme
GRAB GRAB
FWAP FWAP
Ahh...
Wah?
OHHHHHH
NO! NO!
NUH-UH NUH-UH
MY DESIRES COME LAST!
I WON'T SPEND MY MONEY ON DRESSING UP!
BE-CAUSE...
...EVEN IF I CAN'T BECOME A PRIN-CESS...
...I'M—
THE...

Sidebar 1
Oh no!

Something came up that could have been a problem. Well, there was a manga with a very similar poignant story... I thought, "Oh no!! Someone did it first!!" How about the rough school-based story that I had written down as an idea for a one-shot when I was still doing Kurepara? There weren't any other ideas I could do as a series... (Actually, there were, but they weren't suited for Hana to Yume... and there were even ideas that the editor-in-chief told me were "not in style, so wait 5 more years"... So, the school-based story was the one that looked as if it would work for Hana to Yume...But I didn't have the courage or spirit to do that story at that time. I was stuck, so I consulted the editor-in-chief, and received the advice "Why don't you change the setting?" When I took the school-based story's good parts (a school with a performance arts course and the settings for each character), and thought of an interesting "setting," I could only think up a showbiz-based story... I don't have that much interest in showbiz, and don't become a passionate fan of celebrities...

Continued on page 33.

SHOOOO?!
SLAM
DASH
Huh?
...LIVING...
....
HEY ...

...DON'T SAY MY NAME SO LOUD!
I've told you before!
WHAT IF THE NEIGH-BORS NOTICE!

...HAPPILY...
poster
UM...
I'm sorry... I just happened to...
Because I was happy.
...WITH THE PRINCE...

SHO AND I...
All right, let's go!
Yes, sir!
...WERE CHILDHOOD FRIENDS.

I OFTEN STAYED AT SHO'S PLACE GROWING UP, BECAUSE OF MY FAMILY SITUATION.

SO I BASICALLY GREW UP WITH SHO.

We were one in body and spirit!

...UNDERSTAND MORE THAN ANYONE WHAT...
SHO, DID YOU HAVE DINNER?

...TO SAY TO MAKE SHO HAPPY!

SHOULD I MAKE SOME-THING RIGHT AWAY?

OF COURSE I'VE EATEN!

IT'S ALREADY 11!

Shove Shove

...

You're right.

YES ...

She hasn't eaten yet.

...WHY ISN'T THERE ANY BEER IN THE FRIDGE?

HUH?

You're no use to me.

Because...

I... DON'T DRINK BEER ...

And...

CHAK

HEY...

...YOUR CELL PHONE ALWAYS FORWARDS MY CALLS TO THE MESSAGING SERVICE ...
...AND YOU WON'T TELL ME WHEN YOU'RE COMING HOME, SHO...
GLARE
SO IT'S MY FAULT, HUH?

I'M BUSY!

I DON'T HAVE TIME TO CALL YOU FOR THINGS LIKE THAT!

YES ...
You're right...

YOU'RE ABSO-LUTELY RIGHT...

...SEEMS...

SHO...

...TO BE GET-TING MORE AND MORE SULLEN EVERY TIME HE COMES HOME.

Why ?

WHEN WE'D JUST COME TO TOKYO...

...HE WAS SO NICE...

PM 10:30

Oh Sho, you waited for me to Get Back?
Food she Got from Darumaya.

you were working, and I can't eat without you.
And there's nothing to eat with the rice.

COULD IT BE...

...THAT AS HE GETS FAMOUS, THE AGENCY TELLS HIM TO DO THIS AND THAT...?

SHO HATES BEING TOLD WHAT TO DO.

ALL RIGHT, I'LL GO GET THE SPECIAL ITEM.

YES, IT MUST BE THAT ...

SHO, I'M GOING OUT TO GET SOME STUFF.

I'll Be Back soon.

... BECAUSE HE WANTED TO LIVE HIS OWN LIFE...

...SHO RAN AWAY TO TOKYO...

SHO'S FAMILY...

...OWNS SOME OF THE COUNTRY'S MOST PROMINENT OLD JAPANESE INNS, WITH THE MAIN INN IN KYOTO.
...SO...
SHO IS THE ONLY SON OF THE BRANCH OF THE FAMILY THAT RUNS THE MAIN INN...

...HE HATED THE "MARRY A NICE GIRL, AND TAKE OVER THE INN" LIFE.

NO WAY, I WANT A MORE GLAMOROUS LIFE!

The star of a Japanese inn is the proprietress! Why do I have to hide behind the shadow of a woman!

I'M A GUY WHO'S GONNA BECOME A STAR OF JAPANESE SHOWBIZ!

YOU'RE DREAM-ING AGAIN!

WHEN SHO TALKED WITH HIS PARENTS ABOUT HIS FUTURE, THEY ALWAYS ENDED UP FIGHTING.

SHO, WITH HIS BACK AGAINST THE WALL...

...DECIDED TO GO TO TOKYO TO BECOME A "CELEBRITY," AS SOON AS HE FINISHED JUNIOR HIGH.

IF I STAY HOME ANY LONGER, I'LL BE FORCED TO MARRY THIS GIRL FROM AROUND HERE, A GIRL WHO'S PLAIN AND BORING!

TO BECOME A CELEBRITY HAD BEEN HIS DREAM SINCE HE WAS A CHILD.

THE OTHER DAY, I OVERHEARD MY PARENTS MAKING A LIST OF POTENTIAL CANDIDATES FOR MY WIFE-TO-BE!

Oh no!

I'm scared... there's no time to lose!

I...

...DIDN'T WANT TO SEE SHO GET MARRIED TO SOMEBODY ELSE.

I WAS HAPPY ...

... WILL YOU ...

...COME WITH ME?

...THAT SHO...

...CHOSE ME...

...AND I SAID "YES" WITHOUT HESITATING.

HE CHOSE ME WHEN THERE WERE ALL THOSE OTHER GIRLS AROUND HIM...
He was the vocalist for a band.
AHHHH!
SHOOO
SO...
...IF SHO'S DREAMS ARE GOING TO COME TRUE...
...I...
ha
ha
ha
rustle
rustle
TMP TMP

...CAN PUT ASIDE DOING THINGS FOR MY-SELF...

ZIP

SHO ...
Chak
...ARE YOU GOING OUT AGAIN?
NO...
...I THOUGHT ...
...THAT YOU HAD COME HOME TODAY...

I JUST ...
SHUP
UM ...
...CAME TO GET SOME EXTRA CLOTHES.
N—
NO!
Chak
CREE
NOT WHEN I HAVEN'T SEEN YOU FOR SO LONG!
W-WAIT.
Hey...
I JUST ...

2

I have no desire to keep up with the latest trends, thus I don't have any taste in fashion. A show-biz story... I was very worried whether I would be all right going boldly in that direction? But if I was going to draw it, I didn't want to draw a Cinderella-type story where "One day, due to some chance, someone debuts as a celebrity." I do believe that those types of stories grab the hearts of girls more easily, though...

...So I'm writing as if I'm a know-it-all. Although I made up my mind to write a showbiz-based story, I'm having a very hard time drawing. The storyboards take even more time than Kurepara did. (Although it definitely doesn't look that way...) I'd assumed that the new series would be easier to do, both the storyboards and drawing the series itself... I'm a real fool, so I'm struggling to have people enjoy reading Skip Beat each time. Please enjoy it!

...GOT KLIGO PU☆CCHIN PUDDING FOR YOU!
You don't want it?!
SKREE...

PU☆CCHIN
PUU DINNG!

WELL, I'M FAMOUS NOW RIGHT?
I CAN'T SIMPLY GO TO A SUPERMARKET OR A CONVENIENCE STORE...
A COOL GUY LIKE ME CAN'T ASK SOMEBODY ELSE TO GO BUY PUDDING FOR ME, THAT WOULDN'T BE COOL.
I'm happy...
I haven't had this in a while...
This program is brought to you by...
YEAH, YEAH.

THAT'S RIGHT!
ONE MORE THING TO MAKE SHO HAPPY!
BY THE WAY, SHO...

I'M GLAD HE'S IN A GOOD MOOD NOW...
I succeeded in keeping him from leaving.

WORKS EVERY TIME.
Ha ha...

MS. MARUYAMA, WHO WORKS AT THE SAME PLACE I DO...
...STOPPED BEING A REN TSURUGA FAN, AND IS NOW **YOUR** FAN!
What!
Really?!
Of course, of course.
SHE SAID THAT YOU SING WELL.
HEH.
Way TO GO, man!
I will steal every one of his fans!
Yay, me!
shiver
GOOD!
SOON THE DAY WILL COME WHEN I'LL STEAL THE "COOLEST MALE CELEBRITY" TITLE FROM HIM!!
I'll get you, Ren Tsuruga! You're the thorn in my side!
You're not the coolest guy in all of Japan!
I am!
I SHOULDN'T SAY THAT SHE SAID HE SINGS WELL AND IS **CUTE.**
SHO REALLY WANTS TO BE **COOL.**
Now every-body...
Yes...
...the big guest that everybody's been waiting for!
YAHHHHH
...the #1 most desirable man...
YAHH!
...the guy that everybody admits to being the coolest male celebrity!
FREEZE

Mr. Ren Tsuruga!
YAAAAAA
Hello.
...
....
Look over here! YAHHH!
AHHHH!
Rennnn!
Rennnn!
YAAHHHH!
Well, he really is very popular!
Ha-
HALF THE AUDIENCE MUST BE PLANTS!
....
Ren, you have such long legs!
How long is your inseam?
I've no idea, I've never measured it...

HE MUST BE WEARING "HIMITSU-KUN" THAT ARE AT LEAST 6 INCHES TALL!
Himitsu-kun
Platform shoes.
YAAAHHH!
Your face is so small, too!
Nuh uh!
IT'S HIS HEAD, NOT THE FACE!
HIS HEAD IS SMALL!
HIS BRAIN IS THE SIZE OF A PEA, AND IT MUST RATTLE WHEN IT SHAKES!
In a poll taken by women in their early 20s, you were chosen as the #1 most desirable man...
...and here are the results.
What do you think about this?
OOPS.
#1 Ren Tsuruga
#2 Hiromune Koga
#3 Yuzuru Fukamizu
#4 Reiji Taruyanagi
#5 Masahiro Yoshizawa
#6 Issei Asakura
#7 Sho Fuwa
Tadashi Nakajima
Motonori Akao
ding
BAM!
Kyu
.....
SHO!
PWEEE
shuff shuff
OOOOOO!
SHO, DON'T MIND WHAT THEY SAY!

3 Title

Readers close to my age will think of the same thing if they heard the words "Skip Beat." Actually, I rejected the title many times, as well as the character designs, and when I was thinking about the Nth title, I felt that I wanted to put "Skip" in the title, like "Skip something" or "Something Skip." It sounds fun and foreign. A smart kid "skips" from being a grade-schooler or a junior high-schooler to becoming a college student all of a sudden. Like Kyoko says in the story, becoming a star instantaneously, without experiencing periods of obscurity. I wanted to put "Skip" in the title no matter what... and if "Skip" is there, the next thing is "Beat"... My editor and I brainstormed about whether there was another word to use. The word "beat" has the springing meaning, to "hit, drum" (my personal impression) and to "win against the other party or an opponent"...

Continued on page 61.

FOR WOMEN IN THEIR 20S, YOU'RE TOO YOUNG NOW!
You're only 16.
WHEN YOU TURN 20, LIKE REN TSURUGA ...
YOU THINK I CAN'T COMPETE AGAINST REN TSURUGA AT ALL AT THIS POINT?!
People think I'm a bit older than my real age!
!!
I DIDN'T MEAN IT THAT WAY!
YES YOU DID!
I WANT TO RUN NECK AND NECK WITH THAT GUY NOW!
No...
SHO, WAI—
BAM
....

Well, then something that all your fans want to know...
What type of women do you like?
.....
Well...
...some-one kind...
...and with a deep inner strength.
....
shake
shake
shake
shake
shake
shake
Darn you, Ren Tsuruga!
Go disap-pear some-where!
CRASH!!

Blah
Blah
Blah
BEEP
BEEP
Blah
Blah
Please press the pound key...
...after you have finished recording your message.
BEEEEEP
...
SHO...
I'M SORRY I MADE YOU ANGRY... ...LAST NIGHT.
UM...
...UH...
EVEN IF OTHER GIRLS DON'T UNDERSTAND...
...I DO.
FOR ME...
FOR ME, SHO IS A MILLION TIMES COOLER THAN REN TSURUGA!
...YOU'RE NUMBER ONE, SHO.
cree
....
Well...
I WONDER IF THAT WILL STOP HIM FROM POUTING.
sigh

I CAN'T READ SHO'S EXPRESSIONS OVER THE PHONE, SO I DON'T KNOW IF THAT WORKED...
I'LL GO SEE HIM!
HE'S SUPPOSED TO BE APPEARING ON A LIVE SHOW!
Ms. Maruyama mentioned it!
OH, I KNOW!
Today's the second Wednesday of the month!
Daru-maya is closed today.
Blah
Blah
Blah
Blah
Blah
Blah
Blah
WOW...
I'm sur-prised...
I WILL DO IT TODAY!
Blah
Blah
Fight-ing spirit!
Blah
I'll find out where Sho lives...
I called a taxi.
I WILL TOUCH SHO FOR SURE!
...
ALL THESE GIRLS...
wonder if they're waiting for the singers to come out of the studio...
THAT CROWD OVER THERE IS ALL SHO'S FANS.
...
IT MAKES ME...
...KINDA EMBAR-RASSED.

Um... uh...
Excuse me, I have a delivery...
...for Mr. Fuwa.
Specially.
BECAUSE I...
...NATURALLY...
...IN THE PAST, AND EVEN NOW...
Yay, I managed to get through!
I'm glad I'm working as a Moz Girl!
CLIP CLOP
...I CAN BE IN A PLACE WHERE I CAN TOUCH SHO!

I CAN EXPECT...

...A LITTLE...

...BECAUSE SHO CHOSE ME, RIGHT?
SHE SAYS "EVEN IF OTHER GIRLS DON'T UNDERSTAND, I DO."

fwip
fwip
fwip
EVEN IF I'M HER NUMBER ONE...
fwip
fwip
...IT'S NOT WORTH ANYTHING, MAN!
fwip

YOU MAKE HER EARN ALL YOUR LIVING EXPENSES, RIGHT?
THAT'S PRETTY CRUEL.
FWUU
BUT HEY, THAT'S ME!
THE PRINCE OF THE COUNTRY'S MOST PROMINENT JAPANESE INN HAS NEVER CLEANED, DONE THE LAUNDRY, OR COOKED RICE!
HUH?
I'M LIKE A BABY.
DO YOU THINK I COULD HAVE COME TO TOKYO AND LIVED BY MYSELF?!
THAT'S TERRIBLE.
THAT SOUNDS...
...AS IF YOU BROUGHT HER...
...AS YOUR HOUSE-MAID.
HOW...
...CAN YOU SAY SUCH A THING?

KYOKO...
WELL...
...SINCE I WAS A KID, SHE WAS BASICALLY A HOUSE-MAID TO ME.
She used to help out a lot with the inn, and she did what I told her.
OR ELSE ...
...WILL YOU...
...COME WITH ME?
...I WOULDN'T HAVE CHOSEN HER TO COME IN THE FIRST PLACE.

EVEN...
AND I DIDN'T FORCE HER, YOU KNOW?
...IF SHE'S WEARING TATTERED CLOTHES...
...AND IS UN-HAPPY...
I ASKED, "WILL YOU COME WITH ME?"
...AS A QUESTION...
...AND GAVE HER THE FREEDOM TO CHOOSE.
...IN THE END SHE BECOMES MORE BEAUTIFUL THAN ANYBODY...
SHE DECIDED TO COME ON HER OWN...
Cosmetics
...AND IS LOVED BY EVERY-ONE...
AM 12:00
...SO...
...AND LIVES HAPPILY WITH THE PRINCE.
...OF COURSE SHE'S GOTTA WORK HER BUTT OFF TO SUPPORT ME!
I don't want to work outside of showbiz to make money...

Since ...
...You can make enough money to support yourself now...
...Why don't you set her free?
She's not even attending high school, right?
While you have the agency pay for you to go to school.
?!!
Okay, I'll send her back to Kyoto... Fine.
...If you'll take care of me instead of her, Shoko. ♡
Actu-ally...
I'm already being forced to do that! You practically live in my place, and hardly ever go home.
You keep saying that it's my duty as a manager to take care of you!
PLONK
Because I...
KA
SHIK

...LIKE WOMEN LIKE YOU, SHOKO.
Sexy dyna-mite!
SHOCK
SHIK
SHIK
SHIK
SHIK
SHIK
SHIK
SHIK
SHIK
SHIK
BUT ...
...MY PARENTS ...
...IGNORE WHAT I WANT...
...AND TRY TO GET ME TO MARRY KYOKO AND TAKE OVER THE INN.
Just because she's considerate and tactful.
IF I STAY HOME ANY LONGER, I'LL BE FORCED TO MARRY A GIRL FROM AROUND HERE, A GIRL WHO'S PLAIN AND BORING!
NO WAY, MAN!
THAT MEANS ...
EVIL

A GIRL WITH NO SEX APPEAL, WHO DOESN'T EVEN WEAR MAKEUP!
...A GIRL FROM AROUND HERE, WHO'S PLAIN AND BORING.
The prime candidate.
KA SHIK
GREEE

FSSSH
SHUK
THWAK
KOOSH
...
!!
.....
...BUT YOU TOOK ME WITH YOU TO TOKYO...
KYOKO.
WHAT... YOUR CHILD-HOOD FRIEND?!
....
YOU DIDN'T LIKE ME, BECAUSE I WAS PLAIN AND BORING...

... BECAUSE IT WAS CONVENIENT.
.....
WELL...
UH...
SSHHU
....
Sheesh.
DON'T CRY, IT'S ANNOYING!
Darn!
Ha
Ha
Ha
Ha
HEH HEH HEH HEH.
Hee hee hee hee hee hee hee hee.
SMAK
SMAK
SMAK
SMAK
?
KLONK

BWAHAHA
GRUDGE
RESENT
GRUDGE
HATE
AHAHAHA
GYAA!
?!!
SHIFF
For Sho, I can put aside...
...doing things for myself.
Yes, I can!
Ah ha ha!
Sho is my number one!
Hee hee!
SNAP

RAAHHHH!
PWAK
Eeeek!
Nyaa!
Uuu huu huu
FOR ME ...
....
...YOU WERE EVERYTHING!
How DARE you toy with my life!
I loved you so ...
...now I HATE you a million times more!
I hate you ...
I hate you ...
GRUDGE
GRUDGE
GRUDGE
GRUDGE
I...
....
...HATE YOU!!

I'LL HAVE MY RE-VENGE!!
Sha
URK
OH?
YOU?
HAVE RE-VENGE ON ME?
Humph!
HOW?
WHEN YOU CAN'T EVEN TOUCH ME.
Hmph!
HUP
GET HER OUT OF HERE.
Nooooo!
Put me down!
Let me go!
Don't interrupt!
HUP HUP HUP
IT'S USE-LESS.
EACH DAY MY FAME IS INCREAS-ING.
I'M GOING TO BECOME SOME-ONE...
...COM-PLETELY OUT OF THE REACH OF AN ORDINARY, INSIGNI-FICANT PERSON LIKE YOU.
OF COURSE...
Grip
...I'LL NEVER GO BACK TO THAT APART-MENT.

IF YOU WANT YOUR SO-CALLED "REVENGE..."
......
ALTHOUGH ...
...IT'S JUST A WASTE OF TIME FOR YOU.
...JOIN THE BUSI-NESS.
Adieu.
GRRR!
THERE.
Beep!
Beeeep!
Pony PLAZA
VERY

THE BAC...
...LOOKS LIKE THIS.
MISS...
...WITH JUST A NEW HAIRCUT AND HAIR COLOR...
...YOUR IMAGE HAS REALLY CHANGED.
!
Y-YOU'RE RIGHT!
YOU DIDN'T THINK YOU'D CHANGE THIS MUCH, DID YOU?
Ha ha ha!
N-NO!
It's true...
Wahh!...
th-thump
...THAT YOU SHOULD USE MONEY...
For yourself!! hoo
The Truth!
THEN...
...WITH THE BLOW DRY INCLUDED, THE TOTAL WILL BE 24,000 YEN.
KA CHING
FWIP
THANK YOU.
THAT'S 30,000 YEN.
KA CHING
AND YOUR CHANGE...
KEEP THE CHANGE.
...
HUH?
PLEASE...
I'LL...
Heh.
...CO-OPERATE TOO.

I'M IN THE MIDDLE OF...
...DO IT!
TADAH!
...THROWING AWAY MY PAST!
WAIT FOR IT, SHOTARO!
His secret real name.

End of Act 1

Act 2: Once She Haunts You, There's No Stopping It

THE GUY I WAS IN LOVE WITH SINCE I WAS A CHILD...

...DITCHED ME MERCILESSLY, AS IF HE WAS THROWING AWAY SOME USED TISSUE.

IT'S BEEN FIVE DAYS NOW.

I CANCELLED THE LEASE FOR THE EXPENSIVE APARTMENT I RENTED FOR HIM...

...AND NOW...

I'm through with you!
FWAK
AHHH!
Me, covered with so much Sho snot that there are no clean spots left.
trash can

...I'M LIVING AT...
GOOD...

GOOD MORNING!

...

TAI-SHO!
OKAMI-SAN!
... "DARUMAYA," WHERE I WORK EVENINGS.
OH GOOD MORNING, KYOKO.
FOOSH
BOW
HOW ABOUT HAVING BREAKFAST TOGETHER?
UM ...
...uh...
BUT ...
Humph.
munch munch
munch munch
Taisho of Darumaya
OH...
IT'S ALL RIGHT.
DON'T WORRY.
Come eat with us.
Y-YES...
SCHLURP
KLONK
SHUP
UH OH ...
.....
TMP TMP TMP
TAI-SHO ...
Chak
HE'S BEEN LIKE THAT SINCE I DYED MY HAIR...
HE DIDN'T USED TO TALK MUCH ...
But at least he used to greet me...
THAT MAN...

...IS JUST SULKING.
YOU DIDN'T FIDDLE WITH YOUR APPEARANCE, WHICH IS RARE THESE DAYS...
...AND WITH YOUR GOOD MANNERS, HE REALLY LIKED YOU, KYOKO.
He really did.
....
GOOD MANNERS?
I've never thought of myself that way...
TOK
HERE.
Your rice.
Oh!
!
TH-THANK YOU.
BY THE WAY, KYOKO...
I've been wondering about this...
YOU'RE FROM A GOOD FAMILY, AREN'T YOU?
HUH?
OR DOES YOUR FAMILY RUN A LUXURY JAPANESE-STYLE RESTAURANT?
...
NO...
I DID SPEND A LOT OF TIME AT A JAPANESE INN...
But that's Shotaro's place.
...
No?
THAT'S STRANGE.
MY HUSBAND AND I BOTH ASSUMED THAT WAS THE CASE...
It's really not true?
YOUR EASE WITH THE CUSTOMERS AND YOUR ATTENTION TO FOOD IS EXTRAORDINARY.
....
IF I SHOWED THEM THAT SECRET TECHNIQUE I LEARNED BY HELPING OUT AT SHOTARO'S PLACE...
...I WOULDN'T BE ABLE TO DENY IT.
HEY.

Eep!
stir stir
Huh?
Y-
YES?!
TAI-SHO?!
Did he just call me?
ARE YOU GOING TO GO LOOK FOR A JOB...
...TODAY, TOO?
UM...
Y-
YES!
HMPH.
EVEN IF YOU LIE ABOUT YOUR AGE...
...YOU'LL NEVER FIND A JOB...
...IF YOU HAVEN'T EVEN GRADUATED FROM SENIOR HIGH.
STAB
AHHHH!
Wha?
YOU!
You don't have to be so direct!
THERE MUST BE A REASON WHY KYOKO HASN'T ATTENDED SENIOR HIGH!
THE REASON...
shake shake
IF I HAD STAYED IN KYOTO, MY FAMILY WOULD HAVE SENT ME TO SENIOR HIGH AT LEAST...
...THEN I WOULD HAVE BEEN ABLE TO FIND A JOB... OR I COULD HAVE FOUND WORK AT SHOTARO'S PLACE...
FOOSH
FOOSH
BUT...

...IT'S ALL...
...YOUR FAULT, SHOTARO !!!
GRRRR!
I'll never...
...forgive...
...you!
K...
KYOKO ?!
...
Neeever!
YOUR AGENCY SENT YOU TO SCHOOL!
And you didn't tell me!
I'LL NEVER FORGIVE YOU!
blah blah blah blah

4

It's perfect for Kyoko!! My heart throbbed, and the title became "Skip Beat!" Regarding the title—for a long time and up until the last moment, I was thinking about it. So I feel I inconvenienced my editor a lot... The first title I submitted was kinda depressing, and after that I submitted ones that didn't have much effect, or ones people couldn't figure out the meanings of, and they got rejected. And unlike an adult, I complained... (shame) My character designs kept getting rejected too (actually, Ren was rejected, too), and I complained, "Then, what kind of stuff IS acceptable?!" I apologize for being short-tempered. But you, the editor who patiently dealt with me when I had a short fuse, you're a real role model for editors. Thank you so very much.

I will try to watch myself, but I don't know when I may turn out to be a wild horse. So, when that happens, please rein me in.

THESE LAST FEW DAYS, AFTER SHOTARO DITCHED ME...

...I'VE BEEN WANDERING ABOUT THE PLACES WHERE TALENT SCOUTS SUPPOSEDLY HANG OUT...

I'VE TOLD TAISHO AND OKAMISAN THAT I'M LOOKING FOR A DAY JOB AND AN APARTMENT NEAR DARUMAYA.

Blah Blah Blah

...BUT NO ONE'S APPROACHED ME YET.

Sigh...

I WONDER IF MY LOOKS JUST AREN'T ENOUGH?

OF COURSE, IT'S ONLY THE FOURTH DAY...

I WONDER IF I SHOULD AT LEAST WEAR SOME MAKEUP...

I GUESS...

I'LL GO SOMEWHERE ELSE.

...I SHOULDN'T HAVE USED THE MONEY I MADE FROM SELLING ALL MY STUFF...

↑ The Sho Fuwa collection sold for a good price, from CDs to rare items.

...AT THE HAIR SALON AND FOR MY CLOTHES...

↑ And for her shoes and bag.

Uhnn...

NO! NO, NO!!

COSMETICS ARE THE OBJECTS OF MY DESIRE, THINGS THAT I REALLY WANT!

Get a Grip!

Nu-uh Nu-uh

SO I WANT TO BUY THEM WITH THE MONEY I EARN, **CLEAN MONEY!**

I DON'T WANT TO BUY THEM USING THE MONEY I MADE FROM SELLING SHOTARO! THAT WOULD BE LIKE OWING HIM FOR THE COSMETICS!

-Huh??
!!

BY MY-SELF?
THAT'S RIGHT...
THE ROAD TO BECOMING A CELEBRITY IS THE SAME THING!
IF WAITING DOESN'T WORK, I CAN GO SELL MYSELF!
You've got to make the things you want happen!

SHWAA
YES!
A GREAT IDEA!
It must be faster that way, too!
EVEN SHOTARO, WHO CAN'T EVEN USE A VACUUM CLEANER, CAN DO IT.
I MUST BE ABLE TO DO IT TOO!
I GOT BETTER GRADES THAN HE DID, TOO!
This has nothing to do with becoming a celebrity.

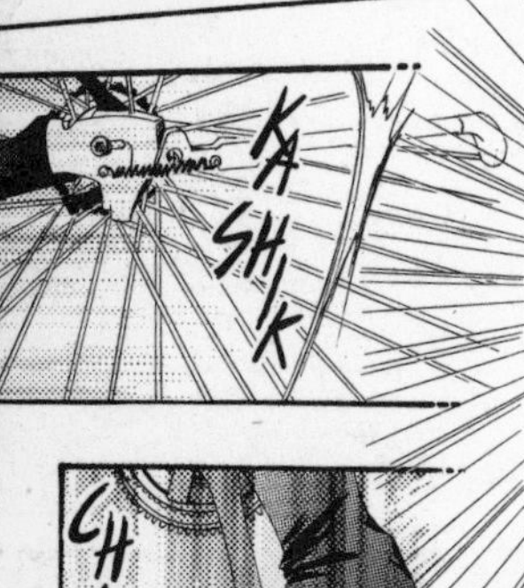
KASHIK

IF I CAN SELL MYSELF TO PEOPLE IN THE BUSI-NESS...
CHAK
...I MAY BE ABLE TO MAKE MY DEBUT FASTER THAN SHOTARO DID!
AND THE DAY I INSTANTLY CATCH UP WITH HIM, THE ONE HE THINKS IS PLAIN AND BORING...
I'll defi-antly do it!
... SHOTARO'S PRIDE WILL BE SHATTERED!

THEN, WHEN HE'S REALLY DOWN, I WILL...
...GIVE HIM A SUPER...
...HURRI-CANE PUNCH FROM THE REAR!
Ahh!
Th-thump
Ah... Ahhhhh!
When I think about that moment...
My heart beats in ecstacy!

JUST WAIT.
Blah whisper Blah
YOU WILL THROW YOURSELF AT MY FEET...
...AND WAIL!
KYA HA HA HA HA!

I will get you, Shotaro!
BWA HA HA HA HA!
SHK SHK
...
I wonder what she's seeing...
I don't think she sees anything...
No...
She only sees the "Shotaro" who's not there.
Poor girl...
And so young...
AH...

Ah...
CHOOO!

HEY! ARE YOU GETTING A COLD ?!
NO PROBLEM, IT'S NOT A COLD.
IT'S JUST SOMEONE GOSSIP-ING ABOUT ME.
GIRLS LIKE ME.
Heh.
As long as there are women in this world, I keep sneezing.
RUMORS ?
IT COULD BE THAT FRIEND OF YOURS, KYOKO, SAYING BAD THINGS ABOUT YOU.
BIP
HUH?
SHOKO, ARE YOU...
... JEALOUS ?
Ha ha!
SHO, WOMEN ARE SCARY WHEN YOU MAKE THEM ANGRY.
Here.
Thanks.
SHE MIGHT REALLY GET INTO THE BUSINESS.
...THAT'S IT'S IIIIIM-POSSIBLE ...
...
IDIOT.
NO WAY.
KSSH
I'VE KNOWN HER LONG ENOUGH TO DECLARE...
Cate-Gorically.
...FOR HER...

...TO MAKE IT IN SHOW-BIZ.
L.M.E. TALENT AGENCY
.....
HUH?
Mukai
SO!
TA DAH
SO!
I WANT TO BECOME A CELEBRITY!
SO PLEASE!
LET ME MEET ONE OF THE AGENCY BIGWIGS!
...
ONE OF THE BIGWIGS?
DO YOU HAVE AN APPOINTMENT?
......
No!
Since I just got the idea about an hour ago!

THEN PLEASE MAKE AN APPOINTMENT, AND COME BACK.
WHAT?!
But I'm here now!
NOBODY'S IN THE OFFICE TODAY?
NO...
THAT'S NOT WHAT I MEAN...
!!!
IF THEY'RE HERE, WHY CAN'T I SEE THEM?!
I THOUGHT TALENT AGENCIES EAGERLY ACCEPT PEOPLE WHO WANT TO BE CELEBRITIES!
WELL... UM...
...
SOMETHING WRONG?
!!
Oh!
MR. SAWARA!
UM...
Blah
Blah
Blah
Blah
HMM.
SO YOU WANT TO BECOME A CELEBRITY.
YES!!
Hmph.
YOU'RE A LIVELY ONE.
THAT'S GOOD.
THEN...
...WHICH SECTION OF OUR AGENCY DO YOU WANT TO JOIN?
HUH?
Section?

A SINGER?
I PREFER LISTENING TO SONGS.
AN ACTRESS?
I HAVE NO INTEREST IN ACTING.
A TALENTO?
THAT SEEMS TOO GEARED FOR VARIETY SHOWS, AND I BASICALLY DON'T WANT TO...
AHHHHHHH!
NOOOOOOO!
WHYYYYY?
No, please stop!
URRRGG!
Exit
REN?!
REN...
...YOU MEAN REN TSURUGA?!
THONK
I UNDERSTAND WHAT YOU CAME HERE FOR!
You're so tenacious!
YOU JUST WANT TO GET CLOSE TO REN, TOO!
Eh?
?!
Huh?!
HE'S PART OF THIS AGENCY?!
Shut up!
DON'T PRETEND AS IF YOU DON'T KNOW!

....
WHAT DO YOU THINK "SHOW" AND "BUSINESS" MEAN?!
It's for those who have the talent to perform and make money!
WHAT'S HAPPENING, MR. SAWARA?
OH.
!!
HISS
AHHHHHH!
Ren Tsurugaaaa!!
He's really here!

?

HUH—

HOW CAN THIS BE?!

GLOOM

OF ALL PEOPLE, REN TSURUGA HAS TO BELONG TO THIS AGENCY?!

SHAKE SHAKE

WHAT, I HAVE TO BE FRIENDS WITH HIM?!

Eyaaa! It's the real Ren!!

Huh? She's not reacting the way I thought she would ...

WHY IS SHE SO CRUSHED BY DESPAIR?

MR. SAWARA, SHE WANTS TO JOIN OUR AGENCY?

YES, BUT...

HUH?

WAIT A MINUTE...

I HAVE NOTHING TO DO WITH SHOTARO ANYMORE...
...so I don't have to hate him.
...SO REN TSURUGA'S NOT MY SWORN ENEMY OR ANYTHING...

SHE DOESN'T SEEM TO CARE THAT MUCH ABOUT SHOWBIZ, BUT SHE WANTS TO BECOME A CELEBRITY.
I SEE.
YUP.

DON'T COME BACK, EVER.
SLAM
OOPS!
How'd this happen?!
She was thrown out.

IN ANY CASE...
...USUALLY, YOU AUDITION FIRST TO GET INTO THIS BUSINESS...
For music, people bring demo tapes or CDs.

I HATE HIM AFTER ALL!
Hey!
It's Ren!
Eyaa!
We were lucky!
REN TSURU-GAAAAA!

...BUT COMING TO THE AGENCY FIRST TO ASK TO BECOME A CELEBRITY...

...HOW ABSURD!

And she has nothing particular that she wants to do!

SHE MUST HAVE COME HERE ON A WHIM.

SHE'LL EVENTUALLY GIVE UP AND GO HOME.

That girl makes no sense at all!!

HEY...

...REN!

There you are!

!

THE EDITOR FROM WILL MAGAZINE IS ALREADY HERE.

ALL RIGHT.

You've got lots of work to do. Do your best!

HOWEVER...

...THREE HOURS...

Blah

Blah

Blah

Blah

What's she doing?

Waiting for a celebrity to come out?

...LATER...

SIGH...

Well, well.

Tap

Tap

Shaka shaka

JOB'S DONE.

CLIP CLOP

I'LL...

...TAKE A BREA—

CLIP CLOP

....

?!

DASH

HUH?!
Blah Blah
Blah
Blah
Blah
...
Hey...
SHE'S BEEN ...
...SITTING LIKE THAT ALL THIS TIME?
THAT GIRL'S BEEN SITTING LIKE THAT, NOT MOVING AT ALL...
MAYBE SHE'S WAITING FOR SOME-BODY.
...I WONDER WHAT SHE'S DOING.
SHE'S A FOOL. STARS DON'T COME IN AND OUT OF THE FRONT EN-TRANCE.
HER EFFORTS ARE USELESS.
......

....
REN!
FSH
TIME TO LEAVE.
Let's GO.
OKAY.
Blah Blah Blah
UH-OH...
...MY LEGS ARE GETTING NUMB...

It's February.
WHOOOO
AND IT'S COLD...
Shiver
I WONDER WHY I'M DOING THIS...
Aching
NUMB
MAYBE I SHOULD GO TO ANOTHER AGENCY.
There's the Ren Tsuruga I hate here, anyway.
N-NO, I CAN'T GIVE UP!
NU-UH!
I must be strong!
IF I JOINED AN AGENCY THAT'S SMALLER THAN SHOTARO'S ...!
UWA HA HA HA HA HA HA!
It's a SMALL agency that suits you perfectly!
A boring girl like you can only GO so far!
Hah hah hah hah!
PAHHH!
THAT TICKS ME OFF!
THEREFORE, THIS IS THE ONLY AGENCY I CAN JOIN!
THIS AGENCY, WHICH ALONG WITH SHOTARO'S, IS ONE OF THE LARGEST AGENCIES!
I'LL GET IN BY ANY MEANS NECES-SARY!!
GRRR!
I can't let that hap-pen!
VROOM
VROOOM
OH?

SHE'S GONE ?

...SHE FINALLY GAVE UP.

OH ...

IT'S ALREADY TEN ANYWAY.

NO MATTER HOW LONG SHE WAITS, THE IMPOSSIBLE IS STILL IMPOSSIBLE...

...I'M GLAD SHE GAVE UP...

I'M LEAVING NOW.

Good-Bye.

GOOD NIGHT, MR. SAWA-RA.

GOOD-BYE.

GOOD ...

GLINT

... BYE.

L.M.E. TALENT AGENCY, TALENTO SECTION SUPERVISOR, TAKENORI SAWARA, AGE 41, BORN MARCH 10TH, BLOOD TYPE AB...

Hee hee...

Lurk

Eyes on the prey.

Peek

She thoroughly investigates her prey.

GYAAAA!

!!!

WH-WHAT, YOU HAVEN'T LEFT?

Th-thump Th-thump

Sh-She surprised me...

NO.

I'VE HEARD THAT IN THE EVENINGS, EMPLOYEES USE THIS BACK EN-TRANCE.

Here.

So I was staking it out.

PLEASE, MR. SAWARA! LET ME JOIN THE TALENTO SECTION!
fsssh
CLIP CLOP
WE SEEM TO BE TOO GEARED TOWARDS VARIETY SHOWS, AND YOU BASICALLY DON'T WANT TO, RIGHT?
I LIED. IT WAS A JOKE.
NO.
I'LL DO ANYTHING.
NO WAY.
FSSH
FSSH
MR. SAWARA.
IT'S ...
... impossible ...
SLAM!
NO!
...FOR YOU !!
VROOOOOM
Mr. Sawara!
OH DEAR ...
She's really persistent.
sigh
BRRRRRMM
I GOT INVOLVED WITH SUCH A WEIR–
Darn.
BLAM

MI...
FSSH FSSH
...SSSS...
...TER...
...SAWARAAAAAAAAAAA!!
FSSH FSSH FSSH FSSH FSSH
GYAAAAAAAH!
Don't follow meee!

BUT...

DING DONG

SAWARA

DING DONG DING DONG DING DONG

A- Are you all right?

Ahh-hhh! Not again!

It's noisy! Stop!

Daughter

Wife

AHHHHHH!

DING DONG DING DONG

...IT CONTINUED THE NEXT DAY...

...AND THE NEXT DAY...

MR. SAWA-RAAAAA, PLEEEASE PLEEEASE.

mumble

LET ME IIIIN, LET ME IIIIN.

mumble

knock knock

LET ME JOIN THE AGENCYYY.

rustle

AHHHHHH!

...AND THE DAY AFTER THAT...
mumble
Mr. Sawara...
You're so mean...
Sound of her scratching the glass with her nails.
SKREEE
SKREEE
I'm pleading, so...
mumble
SKREEE
You're so mean...
SKREEE
You won't even listen to me...
I'll hold a grudge against you...
AHHHHHHH!
Scarrrrryyy!
Noooooo!

...AND IT CONTINUED THE FOLLOWING DAY AS WELL...
I... HAVE... A... GRUDGE... AGAINST... YOU...
FWASH
I'll hate you!
I'll resent you!
UWAWAWA
I'll curse all your descendants!
PUH-
P-puh...

Pleeeeeease...
Pleeease...
...Stopppppp...

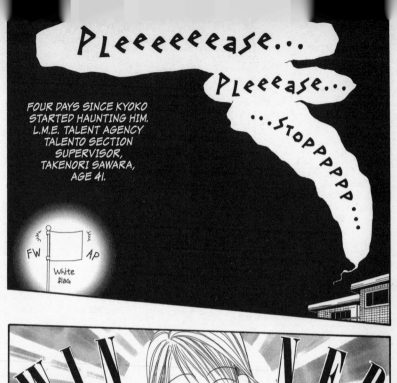

FOUR DAYS SINCE KYOKO STARTED HAUNTING HIM. L.M.E. TALENT AGENCY TALENTO SECTION SUPERVISOR, TAKENORI SAWARA, AGE 41.

White flag
FW
AP

WINNER
No matter...
...how evil the tactics...
...a win...
...is a win!♡
Heh heh!

THANK YOU SO MUCH!
I'LL NEVER FORGET THIS FOR THE REST OF MY LIFE!
BOW
NO...
...DON'T FEEL THAT YOU OWE ME ANY-THING.
Actually, please don't feel that way.
NO... PLEASE LET ME THANK YOU...
BECAUSE NOW...
...I'VE MADE A BREAK-THROUGH IN GETTING CLOSE TO SHOTARO.

....
I SURRENDERED TO YOU FOR A REASON.
A REASON?
I DIDN'T TELL YOU ABOUT THIS, BECAUSE I THOUGHT YOU'D NEVER MAKE IT ANYWAY ...
...BUT THERE IS AN AUDITION TO ENTER OUR AGENCY.
THE AUDITION ENSURES THAT THE CANDIDATES ARE WORTHY OF US.
Hello, this is LME agency.
IF OUR PRESIDENT DOESN'T BELIEVE YOU CAN MAKE IT...
...YOU CANNOT JOIN OUR AGENCY.
OH ...
...I SEE...
THEN I'LL AUDITION TOO!
PLEASE GIVE ME THE DETAILS.
.....
WHY?
WHY IS SHE SO CALM?
She's not reacting ...
...the way I thought she'd react...
Whaaat! I can't believe there's an audition! What should I do?!
WHY...
...IS SHE SMILING?!
The audition for joining our agency?
Ah, you're the one the supervisor was talking about.
Hold on.
Thank you.

DON'T YOU UNDERSTAND?
OF ALL THE CANDIDATES, YOU HAVE THE LEAST AMOUNT OF TIME TO PREPARE FOR THE AUDITION!
Because you came in at the last minute!
SHE...
SHE SCARES ME...
Thank you very much.

clop clop clop clop
ALL RIGHT ...
...THE AUDITION IS ON THE 17TH ...
...I'VE GOT FIVE MORE DAYS.
clop clop
IF I MAKE IT, I WILL...
HEE HEE HEE.
...BE A MEMBER OF THE L.M.E. AGENCY TALENTO SECTION!
She already assumes she'll go there.
ALL RIGHT!
I'LL DO MY BEST!!
BOSH
UMPh.
SHF
....
OWW...
Uh.
FLUTTER
... SORR ...
I'M ...
I...

End of Act 2

Skip·Beat!

Act 3: The Feast of Horror, part 1

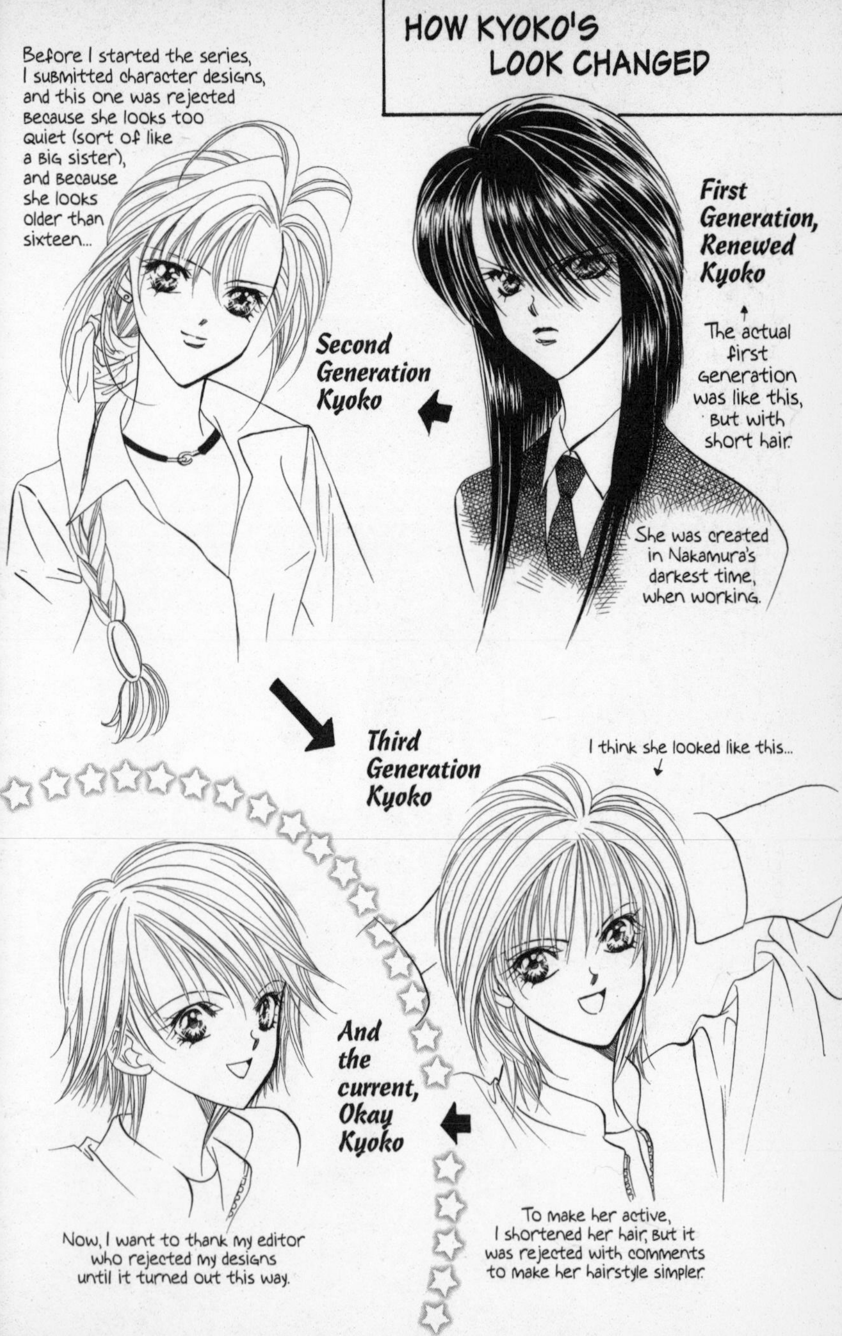

HOW KYOKO'S LOOK CHANGED
First Generation, Renewed Kyoko
The actual first generation was like this, but with short hair.
She was created in Nakamura's darkest time, when working.
Second Generation Kyoko
Before I started the series, I submitted character designs, and this one was rejected because she looks too quiet (sort of like a big sister), and because she looks older than sixteen...
Third Generation Kyoko
I think she looked like this...
To make her active, I shortened her hair, but it was rejected with comments to make her hairstyle simpler.
And the current, Okay Kyoko
Now, I want to thank my editor who rejected my designs until it turned out this way.

PU☆CCHIN

PUU DINNG!

...REN TSURUGA!
NEW-COMERS AUDITION...
...HMM...
Audition
SHIF
MR. SAWARA...
...GAVE IN TO YOU.
tremble
....
I don't like this...
Um...
UH...
My application...
HE'S PROBABLY GOING TO MAKE NASTY COMMENTS...
stare
OOPS.
fwish
glance
!
Eep!
WHY'S HE SIGHING?!
H-how rude!
URK
Sigh
shake shake
WH-
WH-
WHAT'S WITH THAT SIGH, AS IF IT'S JUST A WASTE OF MY TIME TO EVEN TRY, AND I'M GOING TO FAIL THE AUDITION AND REGRET IT?!

WOW, ARE YOU A PSYCHIC?
Can you read minds?
Or is it psychometry?
Grrr!
ANYBODY CAN UNDERSTAND YOU, YOU'RE SO OBVIOUS!
It's not mind reading or psychometry!
I... I...
Snort
Because...
I'M SURE I CAN MAKE IT!
...DON'T THINK TRYING IS A WASTE OF MY TIME!
YOU DON'T UNDERSTAND.
IT'S NOT JUST YOU WASTING YOUR TIME.
THE JUDGES WHO HAVE TO PUT UP WITH YOU THINK IT'S A WASTE OF THEIR TIME, TOO.
They're busy, sheesh.
....
Speechless
HOW RUDE CAN HE BE?!
LIKING THIS BUSINESS IS NOT ENOUGH.
BUT...
...YOU WANT TO JOIN WHEN YOU DON'T EVEN LIKE SHOW BUSINESS.
URK
Well...
...yeah...
...my motives aren't pure...
WHY DO YOU WANT TO JOIN THIS BUSINESS?
THERE MUST BE A REASON, IF YOU MADE MR. SAWARA GIVE IN TO YOU.
ARE YOU JUST CURIOUS?
Hmph!
Hmph
OR DO YOU JUST WANT SOME EXCITEMENT?

I WANT MY RE- VENGE ...
... AGAINST SHO FUWA !!
DON'T ...
YOU GOT ANY PROBLEMS WITH THAT ?!

...THINK I'M JUST ANOTHER HIGH SCHOOL GIRL WITH TOO MUCH TIME ON HER HANDS!
....
SNORT
TAKE THAT!
You've made so much fun of me!
FU—
FUWA, FUWA, WHERE IS IT ?
bip bip bip bip
Accessing the Internet on his cell phone.
Why do you have to look it up?! It's Sho Fuwa! You must've heard of him! He's popular now! A really popular musician! He's a genius who made No.1 on the Oricon Chart with his debut single!!
Why do I have to praise him so much ?!
Ahhhhhhh!
THWUNK THWUNK
I can't believe I called him a genius! I'm such a fool!
pause
....
...
peek
...
WELL ...
OH...
...HIM.
...WITH SOMEONE LIKE HIM, YOU CAN GET YOUR REVENGE IF YOU CAN SING.
Heh!
PAT

WITH SOME-ONE LIKE HIM?!
You...
...laughed!
YOU DON'T TAKE HIM SERIOUSLY AT ALL!
Darn... it...
Ahhh!
GRRRRRR
THAT'S ...
... ONLY ...
...IF YOU PASS THE AUDITION.
STAB
RRR
I'LL MAKE IT! I'LL MAKE IT!!
I'll make it for sure!
RAGING
DON'T BE SO SURE...
AN AUDITION IS DIFFERENT FROM JUST MAKING MR. SAWARA GIVE IN.
DON'T BELIEVE ...
SHUUU
...THAT GUTS ARE EVERY-THING...

Eek!
WH-
WHAT IS THIS ?!

WELL ...
...IN ANY CASE ...
...I WON'T BE ABLE TO CONVINCE YOU...
Heh.
WAIT ...
...SO USE YOUR GUTS...
HUH ?
I THOUGHT ...
...HE WAS BEING REALLY MEAN.
DID I IMAGINE IT ?
...DO YOUR BEST...
...AND GET YOUR EGO SHATTERED.
Halfway to your Goal.
HE DOES ...
Here.
fwip
I won't shatter !!
...SAY THINGS THAT MAKE ME ANGRY...
...BUT...
...ALTHOUGH I FEEL HOSTILE TOWARDS REN TSURUGA BECAUSE OF HOW HE ACTED WHEN WE FIRST MET...
...THERE AREN'T ANY REASONS FOR HIM TO FEEL HOSTILE TOWARDS ME!
No, it makes no sense!
HMPH.
2:35 A.M.
"DON'T BELIEVE THAT GUTS ARE EVERYTHING"!
Who does he think he is ?!
YOU THINK THAT SCARED ME ?!
She was scared.
Scribble
HMPH!
Audition application form.

WHAT'S SO SPECIAL ABOUT SHOW BUSI-NESS ?!
WHO DOES HE THINK HE IS ?!
Don't think that everyone who sees a celebrity gets all excited, and worships you, Ren Tsuruga-aaaaaa!!
SHA
Shoom
thumb-tack
YOU'RE HUMAN, JUST LIKE ME!
WAIT FOR ME, REN TSURU-GA!
I'LL MAKE MY DEBUT REALLY FAST, AND SKIP TO STARDOM IN AN INSTANT!
I won't spend any time in obscu-rity.
Bwa ha ha!
CHAK
She clipped this from a magazine left by a Darumaya customer.
CHAK
AND YOU'LL STAND SIDE-BY-SIDE WITH THIS DORK AND SAY...
... THIS !!
BAM

This poster came with a magazine that a customer gave her.
Sho Fuwa
GYAAAI!
Mistress Kyoko, we completely underestimated you!
Make me your minion!
Make me your slave!
The poster size is in the size of Kyoko's grudge against them.
Bwahahahaha!
Oh my, this is fun and delight-ful!
This is great! Great! Repeat what you said!
HA HA HAHA HA
The room next door
HEY... KYOKO IS LAUGHING REALLY LOUD, ALL ALONE...
And she's talking to someone... ...so late at night...
Th-thump Th-thump
....
It's a bit scary...
IN ANY CASE...
...THE DAY FINALLY CAME.
THE DAY TO CELEBRATE THE OPENING OF KYOKO'S MAGNIFICENT REVENGE PLAY...

5

I will not make any excuses.

Usually, when drawing manga, you have the editor check your penciling, then you do the inking (But...most mangakas probably do the inking without waiting for editors to respond...Because there's no time. ⁶)

I have been doing that for many years since I've become a mangaka, and that day, I sent in my penciled pages as usual. They were the penciling for the last story in this volume, "Act 5: The Emotion She Lacks." My editor looked at it, and phoned me as usual. And after we talked about the things he had checked, he suddenly said, "Ms. Nakamura, who's your favorite Skip Beat character?"

...I'm not the type to "love" my characters, and being asked my favorite when I've just started a series (only Kyoko and Sho have some personality...) I don't dislike Kyoko as a female character, so I can say I like her. As a reader, Sho is someone I definitely...

Continued on page 129

...THE DAY OF THE AUDITION.
LME Talent Agency
27th Newcomers Audition
No. 31-61 Waiting Room
Blah
Blah
Blah
Blah
WUH ...

AWED...
...THIS IS AMAZING...
Blah Blah
Blah Blah Blah
There are a lot...
...MORE GIRLS THAN I'D THOUGHT.
I'VE GOT TO STAND OUT AND GET PICKED BY THE AGENCY PRESIDENT.
Wow!
ALL THESE BEAUTIFUL GIRLS!
Sparkle
Shine
BECAUSE EVERYONE WANTS TO BE A CELEBRITY, ALL THE GIRLS HAVE PUT ON MAKEUP REALLY NICELY.
Wow...
...Beautiful...
WHAT AM I SAYING?!
I shouldn't be ogling at them and sighing!
I'M ALREADY LOST IN THE CROWD!
Ah ha ha!
Ha ha ha!
Twinkle
Fading

THIS ISN'T FAIR! OF COURSE GIRLS WEARING MAKEUP ARE GOING TO LOOK MORE CHARMING!!
NOOOOOO!!
They're ahead of me even before the game's begun!
But of course! Just because I don't wear makeup (don't know how to put it on) doesn't mean that other people won't, too!
IF THIS AUDITION WAS HELD NEXT MONTH...
Oh... darn it...
...THEN I'D RECEIVE MY PAYCHECK FROM DARUMAYA AT THE END OF THIS MONTH!
Why is the timing so bad?!
Is it Shotaro's curse?
He's just Shotaro, and he put a curse on me?!
GRR GRR
RRR
PISSES ME OFF!
To curse someone, I probably need to put some of his hair in the doll...
mutter
snik snik
She actually wants a straw doll or a wax doll, but she can't afford it, so she's trying to make one herself.
She borrowed a sewing set from Darumaya's Okamisan.
HER FUN NEW HOBBY.
Mo!
WHO BROUGHT A KID LIKE THIS HERE?!
I'M HERE RISKING MY LIFE FOR THIS AUDITION!
Blah Blah
Blah
Blah
YOU CAN'T BE PLAIN IN A PLACE LIKE THIS, WHERE YOU EAT OR GET EATEN!
I'll lose my concentration! Mo!
She really keeps saying "Mo."

WHERE'S HER MOTHER? HUH?
FWIP
SPARKS
HUH?
EEP!
.....
SHE'S NOT MY KID!!
Get OUT of my SIGHT!!
She threw her...
She threw her!
She threw the kid!
What a mean woman!

OF COURSE I KNOW THAT!
BUT A YOUNG GIRL LIKE YOU, DOING NEEDLEWORK!
ARE YOU AUDITIONING TO BE A HOUSEWIFE OR SOME-THING?
Oh dear! You're too plain! Stop stop stop stop stop! Mo!
YOU SHOULD BE TENSE AND FIRED UP HERE!
DON'T REMIND ME OF DAILY LIFE!
YOU'RE MISERABLE!
AN EYESORE!
I'M IRRITATED JUST WATCHING YOU!
WHA ...?
So you GO ON and disap-pear WITH THAT kid!
You don't belong here!
SHA
...DO I HAVE TO HAVE SOMEONE I'VE JUST MET, WHOSE NAME I DON'T EVEN KNOW, SAY SUCH THINGS TO ME...
WHY ...
I was just making a curse doll...
I...
...DON'T WANT TO LOSE AGAINST THAT GIRL!
Yeah!!
WHAT'S WRONG WITH NOT WEARING MAKEUP ?!
NO!
MAKEUP DOESN'T DETERMINE CHARM!
ARE YOU ALL RIGHT?
DID YOU GET LOST, LITTLE GIRL?
WHERE'S YOUR MOM?

EVERY-ONE HAS A WEAPON.
Or did you come with your BIG sis?
Can you say your name?
SOB SOB
BOO hoo
I think there was another waiting room.
For numbers 1 through 30.
Maybe she belongs there?
BOO hoo
SOB SOB
IT IS ...
....
Myaa
!!
aah
Yikes!
!!
!!!
...THE HOLY LIGHT THAT RADIATES FROM WITHIN ALL HUMANS...
WHA ...?
Sh-
Ahhh!
WHAT'RE YOU DOING ?!
SHE'S CRY-ING!
There's a mean woman here, too!
IS SHE A DEVIL ?!

...CALLED THE AURA!!
VWUUM VWUUM
LITTLE GIRL...
Apparently, this is a holy weapon that humans are born with.
EEP!
What the...?!
SHE'S RADIATING SOMETHING EVIL!
BWA HA HA
...DO YOU BELIEVE...
...THAT A WOMAN...
...OR A CHILD...
...CAN ALWAYS GET HELP BY CRYING?

Shwap
SIGH...
WE'VE FIIIIIIINALLY FINISHED THE PRELIMINARIES FOR NUMBERS 1 THROUGH 30. WE'RE HALF DONE.
Well, well.
Uhhh.
DON'T RELAX YET, WE'RE STILL ONLY HALF DONE.
Excuse me.
Actors Section →
BUT THERE WEREN'T THAT MANY GIRLS THAT STRUCK ME.
Singers Section ←
OH REALLY? THERE WERE QUITE A FEW GIRLS WE WANT.
I KNOW.
No 31
No 51
flip flip flip
flip
NO... THAT'S NOT WHAT I MEANT...
No 61
...YOU KNOW...
...PEOPLE WHO BECOME STARS HAVE A CERTAIN SOMETHING, EVEN WHEN THEY'RE STILL AMATEURS.
THEIR AURA.
.....
Audition
No 61
Name Mogami, Kyoko
Address 110-006 Tokyo-to
AH.
Actor Singer Artist Talento
HEEEEEY.
DIDN'T YOU HAVE A BETTER PICTURE?
YOU SHOULD BE SMILING IN YOUR HEADSHOT!
She's scowling!
She took the photo with (cheap) a disposable camera, so most of the shots were out of focus, and the ones that were passable all looked like this (because she was desperate). →

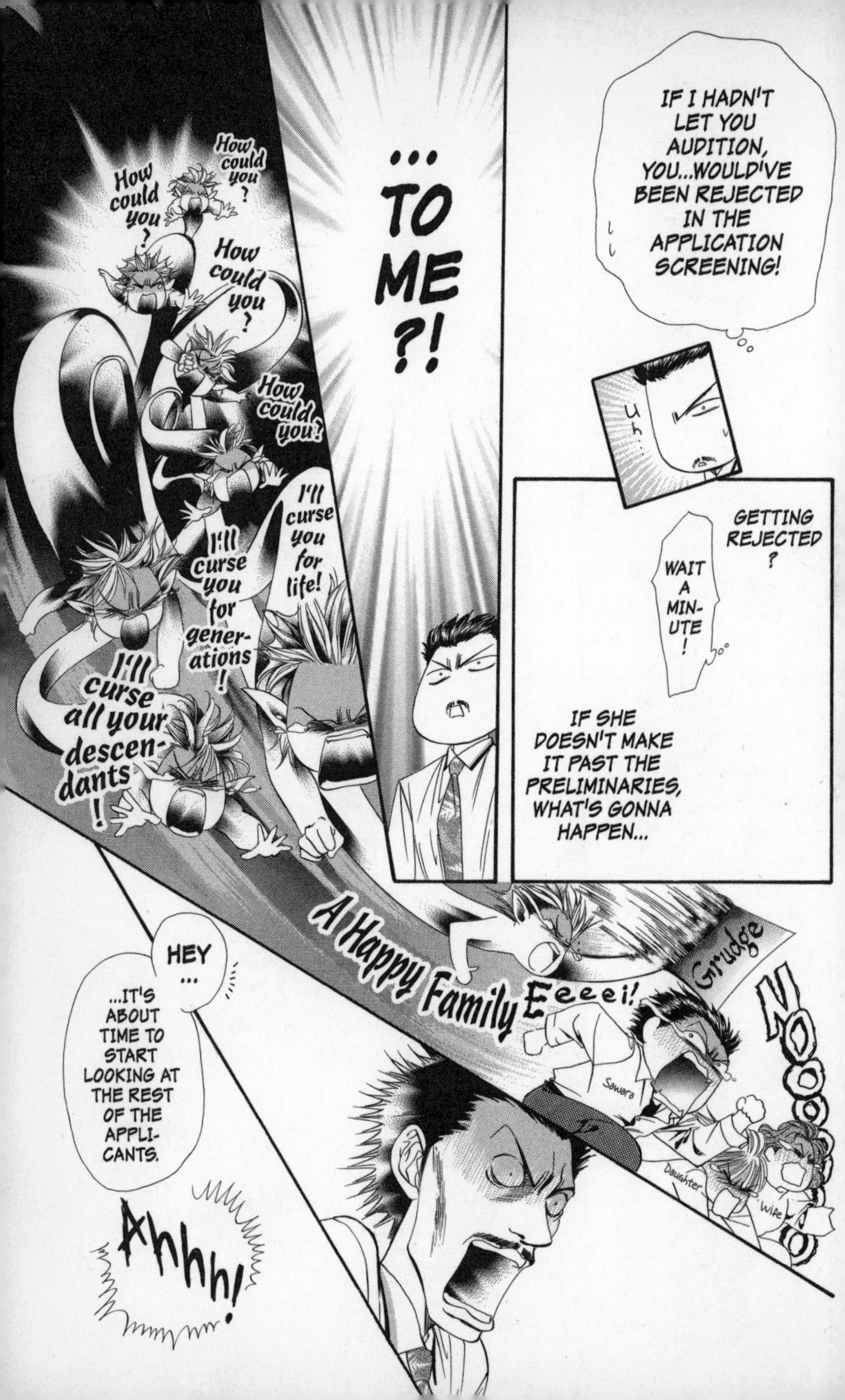

IF I HADN'T LET YOU AUDITION, YOU...WOULD'VE BEEN REJECTED IN THE APPLICATION SCREENING!
Uh...
...TO ME ?!
How could you?
How could you?
How could you?
How could you?
GETTING REJECTED?
WAIT A MIN-UTE!
IF SHE DOESN'T MAKE IT PAST THE PRELIMINARIES, WHAT'S GONNA HAPPEN...
I'll curse you for life!
I'll curse you for gener-ations!
I'll curse all your descen-dants!
A Happy Family Eeeei!
Grudge
NOOOOOOO
Sawara
Daughter
Wife
HEY...
...IT'S ABOUT TIME TO START LOOKING AT THE REST OF THE APPLI-CANTS.
Ahhh!

I'LL GO GET APPLICANTS 31 THROUGH 61.
EE...
THANKS.
EVERY-BODY ...
... FOLLOW ME TO THE AUDITION HALL.
Hmph.
IT'S FINALLY TIME FOR ME TO GO! I WAS GETTING TIRED OF WAITING!
EYAAA!
PLEASE WAIT A SEC!
I-I'M NOT READY YET!!
chatter
Hiee...
IT'S FINALLY TIME!
What should I do?
I'M SO NER-VOUS ...
Blah Blah
clench

PLEASE LINE UP ACCORDING TO YOUR NUMBERS, TWO TO A ROW.
Blah
Blah
Blah
Blah
....
IT'S TIME AT LAST!
Okay...
Blah
Blah
Blah
Blah
peek
....
Hee...

... ABOUT TIME FOR THE SECOND HALF TO START ...

WHAT ?

Blah
Blah
chatter
WHAT'S GOING TO START ?
Scene 21 is set!
...
THE SECOND HALF.

?
WHAT SECOND HALF ?
THE AGENCY AUDI-TION.

I'M SUR-PRISED ...

...THAT YOU WANT TO KNOW HOW THE AUDITION'S GOING.

Every year, you realize that there was an audition AFTER the new-comers make their debut.

IS THERE SOMEONE YOU'RE CURIOUS ABOUT?

....
WELL ...
...IN A WAY, YES.
"REVENGE"...
HOW LONG CAN SHE SURVIVE WITH...

... SUCH AN UNBE-LIEV-ABLE REA-SON ?

And at the very end...
...became independent from LME recently...
WHERE'S THE AGENCY PRESI-DENT ?!
Mr. Sawara, who has a blank look.
Bigwig of Actors Section
Bigwig of Singers Section
Don't care who he is, since he's gone independent from LME.
?!
WAIT A MINUTE!
THE MOST IMPOR-TANT GUY ISN'T HERE !!!
SHABOOOOOOM
AHHHHHHHHHH!!

SSH SSH SSH SSH
WHA ...?
WHA ...?
SHHUK
LA LA LA LA LA LA LA LA LA LA LA LA LA LA
SHAKASHAK
-A LA LA
TOOM TA TOOM TA TOOM TA

FWISH FWISH FWISH FWISH
SHAA
SHAAA
LA LA LA LA LA LA

SHAKA SHAKA SHAKA
SHAKA SHAKA SHAKA
TOOM TOOM
SHIIK SHIIK SHIIK
TOOM TOOM
SHIIK SHIIK
LA LA LA
SHAKA SHAKA SHAKA
SHAKA SHAKA SHAKA
LA LA LA
Pii Pi Pi
Pii Pi Pi
HAAAA BO!
...
FRO——ZEN...
...
...
...
...
...
WHAT... IS THIS?
Their hips move so unbelievably, you can't help but stare.
...
AND ...
...I'M CURIOUS ...
AMONG THE PASSIONATE WOMEN...
HYA LA LA LA
SWISH
... DANCING AS IF HE'S SWIMMING...
LA LA LAAAAAAAA
FWIP
KALACK
...IS THAT MAN ...
LA LA LA LAAAAAA
FWIP FWIP
FWIP
LA LA LA LAAAA

COULD IT BE...
COULD IT BE ...
COULD IT BE ...
COULD IT BE ...
It can't be.
It can't be.
It can't be.
It can't be.
Errrrr...

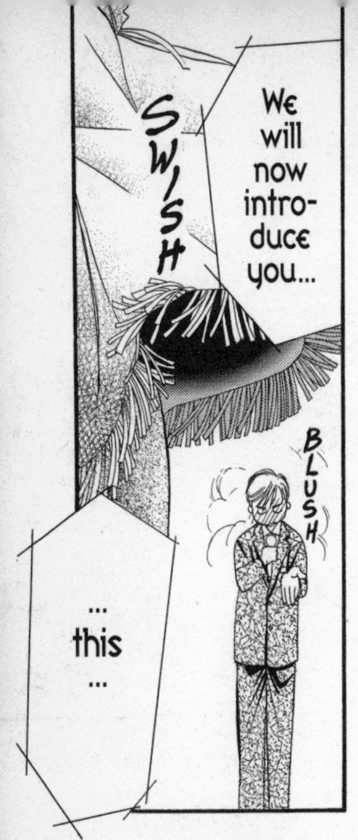
We will now introduce you...
SWISH
BLUSH
... this ...

...is the current president of LME Agency.
SWOOOP
FWIP FWIP FWIP FWIP
...

I'm Lory ...
Really low voice.
His own microphone.
... Takarada.

End of Act 3

AN ...

...AUDITION TO BECOME A CELEBRITY ?!

だるまや

....

THAT... WAS THE JOB YOU WERE LOOKING FOR?!

NO, BUT ...

...IT'S CLOSE.

AND, UM ...

SO... I KNOW YOU MAY SAY NO...

...BUT I HAVE A FAVOR TO ASK, TAISHO!

FWAK

?!

I ASKED HIM, KNOWING FULL WELL THAT HE MIGHT SAY NO.

...I'M FINALLY ABLE TO AUDITION ...

Sha
"TO BECOME A CELEBRITY"...
No. 51.
I will play the violin.
I BELIEVED...
...THAT TAISHO MIGHT THINK I WAS JUST BEING FRIVOLOUS, BUT...
...HE ACTUALLY...
I'LL BE ALL RIGHT.
...LENT ME THIS, SOMETHING THAT'S SO IMPORTANT TO HIM.
IT'S LIKE BORROWING TAISHO'S LIFE.
I WILL...

... PERFORM WELL WITH THIS...

Skip·Beat!

Act 4: The Feast of Horror, part 2

No. 59.
I will...
...tap dance.
New-comers Audition Hall
TAP...
tappity tappity
tappa
shuff shuff
...THIS IS THE THIRD GIRL!
Who tap danced.
Uh!
OH NO, I WON'T STAND OUT AS MUCH!
STOP!
IT'S TOO LATE...
AFTER THE PRESIDENT'S INTRO, NO ONE CAN MAKE AN IMPRESSION ON THE JUDGES.
OH?
BUT THERE WAS ONE GIRL THAT GAVE ME GOOSE BUMPS.
SHE'S AUDITIONING FOR THE SAME SECTION I AM.
THAT GIRL...
Oh!
THAT MEAN GIRL WHO THREW THAT KID!
KANAE KOTONAMI.
Ah!
I WAS SURPRISED AT HER, TOO.
FLIP FLAP
FAWP
I'VE MEMORIZED IT.
Here. Thank you very much.
shu
Oh... thanks.
Wow
...
THEN, UM...
...STARTING ON PAGE 154, THIRD LINE.
Staff from the Actors Section

...

SHAA...

......

WHEN I WALKED THREE BLOCKS...

...I CAME ACROSS A CROWDED AREA WHERE MANY BUSY PEOPLE WERE PASSING BY.

Ooooo!

Blah Blah Blah

WHEN I LOOKED AT THE STREET SIGN, IT WAS APPARENTLY A STREET NAMED BROADWAY...

AND SHE KEPT RECITING, THE WHOLE TIME ALLOTTED.

And she didn't even make one mistake.

THAT WAS EXTRA-ORDINARY.

It's not just a special skill, it's almost super-natural.

Chat Chat

Blah Blah

SHE MUST'VE BEEN THE MOST IMPRES-SIVE...

...OF ALL US.

....

HEH.

OF COURSE.
KANAE KOTONAMI— I WAS BORN TO BE AN ACTRESS!
Ha ha!
I HAVE THE CONFIDENCE...
...WITH THE SPOTLIGHT ON ME, TO WIN THIS AUDITION!
...NUMBER 61.
Ah, I remember her too.
SHE'S HOPELESS.
BECAUSE THE REASON SHE CAME TO THIS AUDITION IS...
OH...
...BUT...
Huh?
...THERE'S ONE MORE GIRL THAT MADE AN IMPRESSION ON ME.
YOU KNOW...
I...
...want to catch up with...
...Sho Fuwa of Akatoki Agency, now!!

I CAN'T BELIEVE SHE SAID THAT.
Hee hee!
Did you see how the judges reacted?
SHE'S SO STUPID!
SHE'S **REALLY** STUPID.
Heh heh

AGENCIES HATE REASONS LIKE "I WANT TO GET CLOSE TO A CELEBRITY" **THE MOST!**

THAT PLAIN GIRL MUST BE AN AMATEUR, SINCE SHE DOESN'T EVEN SEEM TO KNOW THAT.

AND...

I'M...

... ABSOLUTELY SURE ABOUT THIS.

...INSTEAD OF MENTIONING REN TSURUGA, WHO PRETTY MUCH REPRESENTS LME AS A STAR ACTOR...

...SHE MENTIONS SHO FUWA, FROM A RIVAL AGENCY?!

SHE'S NUTS! DOES SHE WANT TO PICK A FIGHT WITH THE JUDGES?!

SHE'LL...

HA!

...BE THE FIRST ONE TO FAIL!

Heh heh heh heh

YES!

SHE'LL BE THE FIRST ONE NOT TO MAKE IT!

Ha ha!

YOU DESERVE IT.

A PLAIN GIRL LIKE YOU, TRYING TO BECOME A CELEBRITY!

UHHHH...

OHHHH...
TH-TH-TH-TH-TH-THAT GIRL!!!
throb throb
throb throb
WHY...
...DID SHE SAY SUCH A THING!
Ahhhhhh!
DID YOU FORGET THAT I ALMOST THREW YOU OUT BECAUSE I THOUGHT YOU WANTED TO JOIN OUR AGENCY JUST TO GET CLOSE TO REN?!
I want to catch up with Sho Fuwa!!
DON'T YOU UNDERSTAND IT'S THE SAME, EVEN IF IT'S SHO FUWA YOU WANT TO GET CLOSE TO?!
Uhhhhh...
OH... NO!
It's...
WELL, WELL, IT'S FINALLY THE LAST GIRL'S TURN.
EEP!
I WAS SOMEWHAT LOOKING FORWARD TO HER, SINCE YOU LET HER AUDITION, MR. SAWARA.
sigh...
YEAH.
BUT SHE'S SIMPLY...
...A GROUPIE.
SHE'S NOT GOING TO MAKE IT!
Ahhh!
sigh...
I DON'T THINK WE CAN EXPECT ANY TALENT FROM HER.
She's probably going to sing a Sho Fuwa song or something.
SHE'S DEFINITELY NOT GONNA MAKE IT!!
I WONDER ABOUT THAT.

!!
?!
IF SHE ...
...WAS SIMPLY SHO FUWA'S GROUPIE ...
CREE
...I THINK SHE'D WANT TO JOIN HIS AGENCY.
PRESI-DENT ...
YOU GUYS ...
...DON'T YOU FEEL THERE'S A DEEP MEANING IN HER ACTIONS?
NOT AT ALL.
NUH UH
THE ...
...PRESI-DENT IS INTER-ESTED IN HER.
Material?
You imagine too much, President.
Hmph. You guys are no fun. Use your imagi-nation!
This is such interesting material!
SH-
SHE ...
Please stop trying to make everyone into characters from a romance.
...MAY MAKE IT!
.....
glance

Number 60
She danced classical Ballet.
huff huff huff
SHWIP
DARN... THERE WAS SO LITTLE TIME, I DIDN'T EVEN GET TO SWEAT.
....
EVERYBODY HAS SUCH FANCY TALENTS.
Piano
Flamenco
Guitar
Flute
and so on.
YOU'RE PLAIN!
MO!
You don't belong here!
SHA
Ah!
WELL, "MOKO'S" TALENT DIDN'T NEED MUCH MONEY!
I saw and heard ...
... more Spanish than English ...
BUT...
...IT...
....
... WAS AMAZING ...
I FELT JEAL-OUS.
NUMBER 61, ARE YOU READY YET?
SHWIP
UM ...
...Y-YES!
I'm coming right away!
IT WAS A TALENT WORTHY OF HER, WHOSE DREAM IS TO BECOME A GREAT ACTRESS.
Personal PR.
MY SPECIAL SKILL...

6

...wouldn't be into, but I can't hate him. I don't dislike him. With Ren, I haven't been able to put forward a firm personality for him, so he's out... Those were the things I was thinking, when the editor answered for me.

It's Lory, isn't it?
!!!

Well, in Act 3, although my schedule was tight, I drew his appearance in great detail, and I did enjoy it a bit. I enjoyed him in Act 4. And in Act 5, towards the very end, although he only appears in three panels, I stopped my hands and pondered many minutes to decide his costume...But...I'd kept it a secret...I'd kept it a secret...!! I thought I'd kept it hidden that I secretly (?) love him!!! (I don't "love" characters I draw?! Geez... And...it's a middle-aged man again...!!) Oh dear (tears).

...It was embarrassingly obvious... " Something's wrong. I had declared that I'd refrain from drawing middle-aged guys...

Continued on page 163

I WONDER...

OH...

...THERE SHE IS.

...HOW FAR I CAN CLIMB...

WHA...?!

WILL THE PRESIDENT...

HUH?

...TAKE NOTICE OF ME?

MANY, MANY PEOPLE...

HUH?

HEY, LOOK.

Blah Blah Blah

...HAD TALENTS THAT MADE PEOPLE SIGH IN ADMIRATION.

I'M...

WHA...?

Erk

...THE LAST ONE.

What the heck is THAT ?!
TA
HI!
Japanese Cleaver
DA
H!
Daikon Radish
TAH
DAH!
61
Barefoot
Atten—
shun!

BWA!
AH HA HA HA!
Oh no!
What is that?!
A daikon?!
What's she GOing to do with it?!
...
Shaking
SHE'S AT IT... AGAIN...
Grrrrr
WHY IS SHE SO PLAIN?!
The atmosphere of the audition is...
IS SHE GOING TO PRETEND TO BE A GROCER?
I'D RATHER SEE HER PRETEND TO BE SHO FUWA.
WHYYYYYYYY?!
Why'd she have to do this?!
CA...
...
BLUSH
AH HA HA HA!
CALM DOWN.
I HAVEN'T...
...DONE THIS TECHNIQUE IN A WHILE...
...SO IF I GET ANY MORE NERVOUS, I WILL DEFINITELY...
...MESS UP...

Oh!
...
NO...
...I WILL SUCCEED...
GRIP
IT'S TAISHO'S ...
...KNIFE.
Okay ...
Ready...
Number 61.
Kyoko Mogami.
HYUP
SHIK
SHIK
SHIK
SHUP
I will make a rose...
...out of this radish.

?!
HUH?!
HYAAAAAAAAAA!
SHUK SHUK
SHUK SHUK
FWIP FWIP FWIP FWIP
SHUK
SHUK
PAWAP
OOOOOOOOOO!
This is the base for the rose. It is made from the thickest part of the radish, which was cut off, then hollowed out.
TH-THIS IS...
...KATSURA-MUKI, THE ART OF VEGETABLE PEELING!

SHUK
SHUK
SHUK
SHUK
SHE'S DOING KATSURA-MUKI, WHICH ONLY A PROFESSIONAL JAPANESE COOK CAN DO!
Who is she?!
SHUK
SHUK
YES, YOU'RE RIGHT.
FSSH FSSH FSSH FSSH
ONLY THE BEST JAPANESE COOKS CAN DO THIS!
THAT'S WHY I TRAINED REALLY HARD SINCE I WAS LITTLE!
Covered with blood
SPLURT
Ends of a radish that was thrown away because it had gone bad.
IT WASN'T BECAUSE I WANTED TO BECOME A JAPANESE COOK!
MOST OF THE YEAR, SHOTARO'S PARENTS TOOK CARE OF ME.
HOW LONG IS KYOKO STAYING THIS YEAR?
I don't know.
SAENA HASN'T CALLED YET...
SO I DIDN'T WANT SHOTARO'S PARENTS TO CONSIDER ME A NUISANCE!
KYOKO IS POPULAR AMONG THE CUSTOMERS.
SHE'S AMAZING.
I'M SO PROUD.
SHE CAN DO KATSURA-MUKI, ALTHOUGH NOT YET PERFECTLY!
SHOULD I HAVE HER TAKE MY PLACE IN THE FUTURE?
Sho's dad is the chef.

... I'M SORRY ...
...IT TURNED OUT TO BE A CABBAGE INSTEAD OF A ROSE...
huff
huff
huff
I GOT CARRIED AWAY AND PEELED TOO MUCH...
That's Beautiful By itself!
Really!
CLAP CLAP
CLAP
Wonder-ful!
You showed us a real crafts-man's skill.

CLAP CLAP CLAP CLAP
....
Well, well, I'm surprised.
You're Great.
That was the most interesting skill of all.
DID...
...I...
...MANAGE TO LEAVE AN IMPRESSION ON THE PRESIDENT ?
glance

AHAAAAA!
I did it!
Way to go!
I DIDN'T THINK ANYTHING I LEARNED AT SHOTARO'S INN WOULD HELP ME HERE!
EVEN THAT FOOL IS A BIT USEFUL SOMETIMES.
Hmph.
BECAUSE THEY WERE SHOTARO'S PARENTS...
...I WAS DESPERATE TO LEARN, SO THEY WOULDN'T HATE ME.
FWISH FWISH
Oh...
Doing all that for the sake of one guy.
I WAS SUCH AN ADMIRING AND STUPID CHILD...
BUT NOW I WANT TO THANK THEM FROM THE BOTTOM OF MY HEART.
To Shotaro's parents, who polished my skills as I grew up.
AND TO...
I...WONDER IF I CAN BELIEVE THAT TAISHO DOESN'T DISLIKE ME?
It's a spare knife...
...But it's been well taken care of, an excellent knife...
It is his knife.
...TAISHO.
It's okay, right?
I'll believe it's okay.
THANK YOU SO MUCH.
RUB RUB

THANKS TO YOU, MY CONFIDENCE, WHICH HAD RUN AWAY FROM HOME, HAS COME BACK!
RAAH!
I'm home! Let's go for it! Really go for it!!
SHOOM
CONFIDENCE
For some reason, it's Shotaro. Because he's over-confident?!
roll roll
Ha ha!
SEE? GUTS ARE ENOUGH TO MAKE IT IN SHOWBIZ.
LOOK AT ME, REN TSURUGA!
DON'T BELIEVE...
...THAT GUTS ARE EVERYTHING...
YOU SAID THAT!
Looking down on me!
How embarrassing!
I WILL BLAZE FORWARD!
I WILL ZOOM PAST THE PRELIMINARIES!
GO!
HEY, YOU.
Blah Blah Blah
Okay then...
...Singer Section, please come this way. Actor and Talento Sections, please follow our instructions and...
!
YOUR RADISH PEELING...

HUH?
... WAS AMAZING.
TH- OH ...
SHOWING OFF A SKILL LIKE THAT...
...AT AN AGENCY AUDITION IS SO UNUSUAL, EVERYONE WILL REMEMBER IT.
HMPH
DON'T BE JEALOUS.
I thought it was strange that she was complimenting me.
I'm NOT JEALOUS!
I wouldn't want to master radish peeling, even if you asked me to!!
DON'T...
... GET ME WRONG.
WHAT?
YOU STOOD OUT FROM THE CROWD ...
...AND I THINK THE PRESIDENT NOTICED YOU, TOO.
BUT THAT'S BECAUSE YOU DON'T BELONG HERE.
You stand out because you don't fit in.
IN OTHER WORDS ...
...YOU'RE A RARE ANIMAL NOT USUALLY SEEN BY HUMANS...
...A DWARF HIPPOPOTAMUS.

R-rare...?! Dwarf...
BUFFOO—
HIPPO-POTA-MUS?!
Dwarf Hippopotamus
A small hippo, just like the name says. It's one of the three rarest animals in the world.
I WILL FORETELL THIS—
Heh heh.
I WILL PASS THIS AUDITION AS THE MOST PROMISING NEW-COMER...
...BUT YOU WILL BE THE FIRST TO FAIL.
Ha ha!
YES ...
... YOU'RE PLAYING ...
... SECOND FIDDLE TO ME.
Grr
SE-
SECOND FIDDLE ?!
GRAAA RAAHH
Every-one will...
...now do a reaction test.
I DO BELIEVE YOUR SPECIAL SKILL WAS AMAZING, BUT...

WHY!
DO I HAVE TO...
...PLAY SECOND FIDDLE TO YOU?!
Please react...
...to the words the person on the cell phone speaks to you.
We'll start with Number 31.
Um ...
Y-Yes!
AND...
...WHY DO I HAVE TO REACT RIGHT AFTER HER?!
She was Number 46, I'm Number 61!
Side-by-side?!
The people auditioning for the Singers Section left, hence the two are side-by-side.
DO ...
... YOU KNOW?
mumble
THAT THE LME AUDITION ACTUALLY STARTS NOW.
WHAT?
THE QUALIFYING ROUND IS THE SAME EVERY YEAR...
...BUT AFTER THAT, IT'S DIFFERENT EVERY YEAR.
THAT'S BE-CAUSE ...
Huh?
What?
Um...
Uh...
UH ...
...

...THE PRESIDENT DECIDES THIS TEST HIMSELF.
!!
IF THE PRESIDENT DOESN'T LIKE YOU...
...HE WILL FAIL YOU WITHOUT MERCY.
THAT'S ONE REASON...

...WHY THE LME AUDITION IS SO DIFFICULT.

Hee hee hee hee

Hee hee hee

hee

...WILL STAY UNTIL EVERYTHING IS OVER...

....

glance

FORTUNATELY, THE PRESIDENT HAS TAKEN AN INTEREST IN YOU.

THE SECOND ROUND OF SCREENING ACTUALLY TESTS PHYSICAL STAMINA.

You were able to overtake a taxi on your bike, so you shouldn't have any problems.

IF YOU PASS THE PRELIMINARIES, YOU'RE ALMOST AT THE DOOR OF SHOW BUSINESS.

PLEASE GOD...

I PRAY THAT THIS SMILE...

SOME-
THING
SIMPLE
IS
ENOUGH.
LISTEN
...
....
Hah!
...BUT DON'T...
...TO THE
WORDS
ON THE
CELL
PHONE...
!
HER
EXPRES-
SION
CHANGED
!

I'M SO HAPPY ...

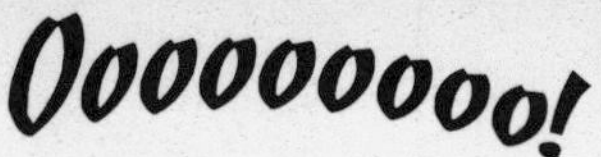
Oooooooooo!

THREE SECONDS AND SHE'S CRYING!
THIS REACTION TEST IS SO SHORT...
...BUT SHE WAS ABLE TO PULL IT OFF.
SHE REALLY IS AMAZING, PRESIDENT!

Wow!
Uh-huh!
Yup yup
....

SH-SHE'S NEXT.

PLEASE ...
Here.
Humph
....
...YOU DON'T NEED TO REACT AS WELL AS...
She's back to normal already.

Number 61.
Kyoko Mogami.
I'm ready to begin.
SHWIP
... KANAE KOTONAMI.
...

SILENCE
?
Huh?
I...
...went out with lots of different women...
WHAT?!
WHAT?
...but they didn't work out.
WHAT?!
I was a fool.
They said they couldn't ...
...stay with me, that I'm too selfish.
TOOM
NYA NYA NYAA
Selfish
Self-centered
Overconfident
Top 3 Pronouns to Describe Shotaro Fuwa

ERRRR
....
SOME-THING SIMPLE IS ENOUGH.
th-thump th-thump
th-thump th-thump
And I finally realized...
...how much...
...you loved me.
GRAAAAAAAAAH
Kyoko Mogami Kaleidoscope of Memories From Her Noble Period
SHO!
LISTEN TO THE WORDS ON THE CELL PHONE ...
I loved only you ...
...from the beginning.
... BUT DON'T ...
I know I'm being selfish.
I'm sorry ...
GRR GRR GRR
But ...
Ah!

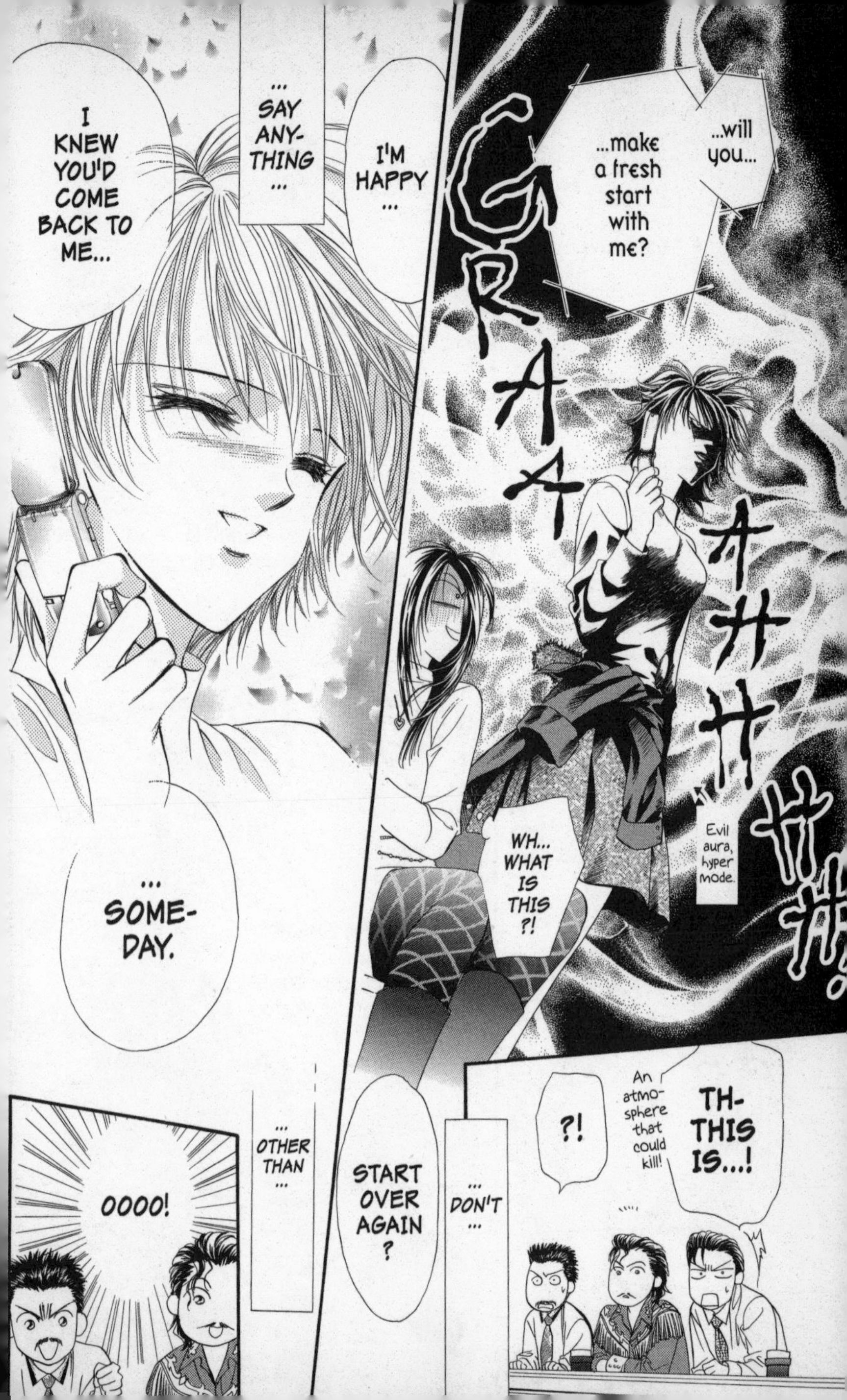
...will you...
...make a fresh start with me?
GRAAAHHHHA!
Evil aura, hyper mode.
WH... WHAT IS THIS?!
I'M HAPPY...
...SAY ANYTHING...
I KNEW YOU'D COME BACK TO ME...
...SOMEDAY.
TH-THIS IS...!
An atmosphere that could kill!
?!
...DON'T...
START OVER AGAIN?
...OTHER THAN...
OOOO!

YOU THOUGHT I REALLY MEANT THAT ?!
You jerk!
IF "SORRY" WAS ENOUGH, THERE'D BE NO NEED FOR HELL!!
BAM
... WORDS ...
EEEK!
SHWIP SHWIP
fling
flang
Cell phone parts
BOUNCE
... OF RECON- CILIA- TION ...
OH ...
Huh?
D...
DARN IT!
I...
I'M SORRY !
...I BROKE THE CELL PHONE ...
flustered
scrabble
HUH ?

AWWW...
PUPPY FACE
Sa... ...lump

End of Act 4

Skip·Beat!
Act 5: The Emotion She Lacks

Applicants Who Passed the First Round

(In the Acting and Talento divisions)

46

11 Passed

31
32
35
37

41
42
43
44
45
46

11 Passed

Blah

Blah

Blah

Blah

......

Blah

Blah

Blah

I'm so glad! I thought I wouldn't make it.

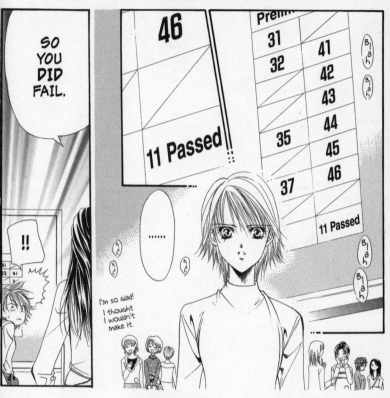

SO YOU DID FAIL.

!!

SO ...
...AS I FORETOLD, RIGHT?
Heh heh!
What is there to be depressed about?
I... I DON'T THINK I FLUNKED BECAUSE THEY COMPARED ME TO YOU!
Oh.
SO WHY DID YOU FAIL?
Everyone who passed the preliminaries, please come into this room...
Oh.
TH- THAT'S ...
... BECAUSE ...
Um... uh...
OH DEAR, I HAVE TO GO.
ABRUPT
She ended the conversation
CLIP CLOP
UM ...
Hey...
I DON'T GET IT...
OH ...
PAUSE
... SINCE ...
... WE'LL NEVER MEET AGAIN ...
GOOD-BYE.
GLEAM
HA HA!
GRR GRR GRR
.....
HA HA HA LA LA LA
WHY ...
... DIDN'T I MAKE IT?

THE PRESIDENT LIKED ME, TOO!

....

I KNEW ...

Sigh

...ooo

... YOU'D COME.

Even if you hide, your evil spirits are circling.

Booooowaaah

I can't go home!

I can't go home!

!!

I can't go home until I know why I failed!

A café in the LME Building

LA. HEARTS

Blah Blah

Blah Blah

Then...

BECAUSE I BROKE THE CELL PHONE!

Yes, that's the only reason I can think of!

THEN I'LL PAY FOR IT, SO...

THE PRESIDENT AND...

...MR. MATSUSHIMA OF THE ACTORS SECTION GAVE YOU HIGH MARKS.

NO...

...THAT HAS NOTHING TO DO WITH IT.

IN YOUR CASE, YOU LACK WHAT IS MOST NECESSARY TO A CELEBRITY.
AND OF ALL THE APPLICANTS WHO FAILED, YOU LACK IT THE MOST.
?!
YOU ...
WHEN YOU HEAR THE WORD "LOVE," WHAT DO YOU THINK OF?
The prelude to despair and destruction !!
Imme-diate Answer.
DEFINITELY!!
....
WHAT ?!
Oh no!
AWWW...
H-Huh ?
LISTEN.
YOU CAN'T BECOME A CELEBRITY JUST BY BEING SELF-SATISFIED.
IF YOU BELIEVE THAT YOU'RE A SUCCESS ONLY BECAUSE **YOU'RE** TALENTED, AND DON'T CARE FOR THE PEOPLE AROUND YOU, THEN YOU'RE NOT A REAL CELEBRITY.
That's just pretend-ing.
A CELEBRITY CAN ONLY BE A CELEBRITY WHEN THE PUBLIC WANTS THEM.
THEY CAN GROW BECAUSE THEY'RE LOVED.

CELEBRITIES CAN FADE AWAY IF THE STAFF HATES THEM.
AND NOT JUST THE PUB-LIC.
THERE-FORE ...
...AS THE PRESI-DENT PUTS IT...
Excuse me.
Ah... Yes.
Coffee, please.
...IF YOU WANT TO SUCCEED AS A PROFES-SIONAL...
...YOU SHOULD ALWAYS REMEMBER TO LOVE YOUR AUDIENCE ...
...AND WANT TO BE LOVED BY THE AUDIENCE!
For you guys, the audience is water and fertilizer!
You should remember that you earn your living by selling dreams to the public!!
SO THAT'S IT.
He always says this.
.....
TO LOVE ...
Well, the last reaction test was a judgment test...
... AND TO WANT ...
... TO BE LOVED ...
...a psycho-logical test about "love" that the President devised.

I...

...WAS OFTEN TOLD THAT AT SHOTARO'S INN.

KYOKO, ONCE YOU'RE IN FRONT OF THE CUSTOMER, YOU MUST ALWAYS SMILE.

NO MATTER HOW ILL YOU MAY BE...

...DON'T SHOW IT.

OUR BUSINESS IS A SUCCESS ONLY WHEN THE CUSTOMER FEELS GLAD THAT THEY CAME, AND THAT THEY WANT TO COME AGAIN.

YOU HAVE TO WANT THE CUSTOMERS TO LOVE OUR INN.

...WE CAN'T FORGET...

...TO LOVE THE CUSTOMERS, TOO.

SHOW BUSINESS...

...so the more forgiving the response in that reaction test...

AT THE SAME TIME...

...IF WE WANT THE CUSTOMERS TO LOVE US...

....

"THE SERVICE INDUSTRY."

...the more that person wants to love and be loved, deep inside their heart.

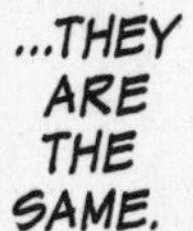

...THEY ARE THE SAME.

OF COURSE, THAT'S WHAT THE PRESIDENT MAINLY CONSIDERS, BUT...
...MR. MATSUSHIMA AND I...
MR. SAWARA...
I...
Huh?
......
WHAT HAPPENED?
.....
I...
...CAN'T DO IT.
...UNDERSTAND.
...
YOU'RE...
...CONVINCED?
I THOUGHT YOU'D BE MORE PERSISTENT...
YOU WERE SO PERSISTENT WHEN YOU WERE STALKING ME.
WHERE'D THAT PERSISTENCE GO?
....

EVEN IF YOU LOVE SOME-ONE...
... THERE'S NO GUARAN-TEE THAT THE PERSON WILL LOVE YOU...
I THREW AWAY MY FUTURE ...
THAT'S TERRI-BLE.
THAT SOUNDS ...
...AS IF YOU BROUGHT HER...
...AS YOUR HOUSE-MAID.
... AND LOVED ...
WELL ...
...BUT NOTH-ING...
...CAME OF IT...
HOW ...

...CAN YOU LOVE...

...PEOPLE...

I...

...THAT YOU'VE NEVER MET, COMPLETE STRANGERS?

...THINK...

......

...ANYBODY.

IF YOU...

...CAME HERE TO BE A TALENTO...

...I'VE LOST THE DESIRE TO LOVE...

...YOU WANTED TO HAVE PEOPLE WATCH YOU...

...AND LOVE YOU...

...RIGHT?

I'VE FOR-GOTTEN ...

...HOW TO WANT...

Hah.

YES...

...TO BE LOVED...

!!

... LONG, LONG AGO ...

Blah
Blah
Blah
Blah
Then that's how we'll pro-ceed.
We'll talk about this later.
Thank you very much.
.....
I...

... TOO ...

... DON'T UNDER-STAND THAT GIRL AT ALL.

SHE CAME AT ME WITH A TENACITY THAT SCARED ME OUT OF MY MIND, SAYING SHE WANTED TO JOIN THIS BUSINESS...

...AND YET SHE ASKS HOW YOU CAN LOVE YOUR FANS.

TOINK
!
!!
GYAA
!!
Heh heh heh!
WHAT HAPPENED, MISTER? YOU'RE HERE ALONE, MAKING SUCH SCARY FACES.
MARIA.
YEEES.
Mister.
Huh?
Oh.
I WAS SO WORRIED, I COULDN'T HELP TALKING TO YOU.
!
OH...
I GET IT.
YOU'RE RELAXED AND HAVING TEA HERE BECAUSE THE RESULTS OF THE AUDITION ARE IN.
HUH?
Well...
Y-YEAH.
Yay!
WHAT HAPPENED TO NUMBER 61?
61
....
THAT GIRL...
MISTER?

POOR GIRL.

SHOULD I...

Mister?!

Hey, tell me what hap-pened!

... LEAVE HER ALONE? WILL SHE BE OKAY?

FOR FOUR DAYS STRAIGHT, SHE PLEAD-ED...
...TO BE ABLE TO AUDITION...
Actually, she stalked and threatened.
OKAMISAN, SOMETHING HAPPENED TO KYOKO?
Blah Blah Blah

HUH?
Well ...
YEAH... YOU KNOW...
...
What, what?
We wanna know.

SHE JUST ...
... TRIPPED AND FELL.
SIZZZZZ

IT'S NOTHING.

DEPRESSED
She doesn't look okay.

1

When I realized that compared to the main, young characters, the ratio of middle-aged guys was going up... Oh nooooooo!! This is becoming like Kurepara!! I'm sorry!! I'm sorry!! I'll stop!! I'll really stop drawing middle-aged guys!! I will try to control myself...waaah!... It's not too late to start now...no more middle-aged guys!! ...But as I say this, I've added a scene where Lory ponders about Kyoko...this is not convincing at all...

I wanted to put this scene when the story was printed in the magazine too, and I couldn't... But... even if I could've put that scene in the magazine, I don't know whether he'd have been dressed like that, and pondering like that...well...in the end, I must love Lory...

...I definitely do not...

...deny it...

Ahhh!

EVERY-ONE DOES THAT.

You guys came here to drink because you had something to be upset about, right?

Oh ...

Yeah.

What was it?

When we eat Taisho's food, we forget why we were upset.

Ah ha ha ha ha

Yeah, yeah! And you make us laugh, Okamisan.

YOU DON'T...

...HAVE TO WORK TODAY.

YOU CAN'T BE IN FRONT OF THE CUSTOMERS LIKE THAT.
FWUMP
I'M SO ASHAMED.
PEOPLE STILL SAY THE SAME THINGS TO ME.

I... MIGHT HAVE NEVER...
FWOOM
... DEALT WITH A CUST-OMER WITH LOVE.
Sigh...
BECAUSE ...

...WHEN I WAS AT SHOTA-RO'S INN...
...
ROLL
ROLL
...I WANTED TO BE PRAISED BY SHOTARO'S MOM, SO I JUST DID WHAT I WAS TOLD TO DO...

EVEN AT DARUMAYA ...

...I WORKED BECAUSE TAISHO AND OKAMISAN LIKED ME.
YES...
IT WASN'T...
... BECAUSE I WANTED THE CUSTO-MERS TO BE HAPPY.
'CUZ I WAS TRYING SO HARD TO MAKE A LIVING IN TOKYO, WITH SHOTARO.
Sho Fuwa
...I DID SOME-THING FOR SOME-BODY...

...ALWAYS, ALWAYS, ONLY FOR THIS GUY.
AND THAT MAKES ME SO SAD!
Ahhh, What was my life for ?!
Don't smile! You good-for-nothing!!
RIIP
...LOST AN IMPORTANT EMOTION !!
SHRED
SHRED
SHRED
SHRED
Because of you, I...
...I...
...I...
SHRED
SHRED
SHRED
SHRED
"LOVING" SOMEONE...
...IS THE MOST WASTEFUL THING ...
"WANTING TO BE LOVED" ...
...YOU CAN DO IN THIS WHOLE WORLD.
... SEEMS ...

...HOPE-LESS...
...THE MORE...
...YOU YEARN FOR IT.
PLIP

IS THAT...

...NECESSARY
TO BECOME A
CELEBRITY?

NO...

.....

IT'S
...

... NECESSARY TO BE A HUMAN BEING.

THAT NIGHT I...

...CRIED, WHICH I HADN'T DONE IN A LONG TIME.

I WAS MAD AT MYSELF...

...I FELT POWERLESS...

...I WAS SAD...

...I COULDN'T HOLD BACK...

...MY CRYING...

...MY TEARS...

...I CRIED...

...LIKE A CHILD...
SWIRL

Hmmm...
....
ROLL ROLL
He's massaging the pressure points of his feet.
Hmmm...
ROLL ROLL ROLL ROLL
....
Objective: Actor Singer Artist Talento
HMMM.
THE PEOPLE WHO RAISED ME WITHOUT SHUNNING ME.
THE PEOPLE WHO GAVE ME A PLACE TO SLEEP, WITHOUT BEGRUDGING IT.
THE PEOPLE I RESPECT.
Shotaro's parents and Darumaya's owners.
IF SHE GOES OUT INTO THE WORLD AS A TALENTO, I'M CURIOUS...
Special Skill
I can cut, peel, and take apart anything.
Favorite Word
Fugutaiten
The feeling of hatred so great, you don't even want to let the person live.
...
She had to pick this word...
THAT GIRL...
HOBBY.
LOOKING AT COSMETICS.
...WHAT SHE'LL DO.
...
...WILL NOT BE ABLE TO GROW...
....
...EVEN IF SHE MAKES HER DEBUT.
BUT...
THIS ISN'T RIGHT...
Of all the girls I've seen so far...
BUT...
I watched her reaction test, and my instincts screamed out.
Briiing

Br-i-i-i-i-n-g
Com-ing.
IT'S YOU ...
...MR. SAWARA.
... I'VE GOT ...
... SOME-THING HERE ?
CHIRP CHIRP CHIRP
SHOULD I LET HER GO ?
HELLO ?
HUH ?
Oh.
WHEN I FEEL...
What hap-pened ?
...
She's eaves-dropping.
NOD
...
SHE'D SHRIVEL UP IF SHE CRIED THAT MUCH ALL NIGHT...
I felt so sorry for her, she was trying not to let any-one hear her cry.
I should've had her drink some sake.
SILENCE
TAK TOK TAK TOK
KYOKO ...
... SEEMS TO HAVE CALMED DOWN.
...
....

CHIRP
CHIRP
CHIRP
CHIRP
....
IT'S MORNING...
I...

...COULDN'T SLEEP AT ALL...
Exhausted
Err
...I'M TIRED...

I...
...HAVEN'T CRIED THIS HARD IN A LONG TIME.
I USED TO CRY A LOT WHEN I WAS LITTLE.
I THOUGHT IF I CRIED...

...SOMEBODY...
...WOULD...

—ther...

MOTHEEER...
...HELP ME...

....
BUT ...
...IN REALITY...
SHWIP
....
THE STONE ...
... that stone ...
Yes ...
DIG DIG DIG
It's not here. No.
It's in this BAG.
DIG DIG

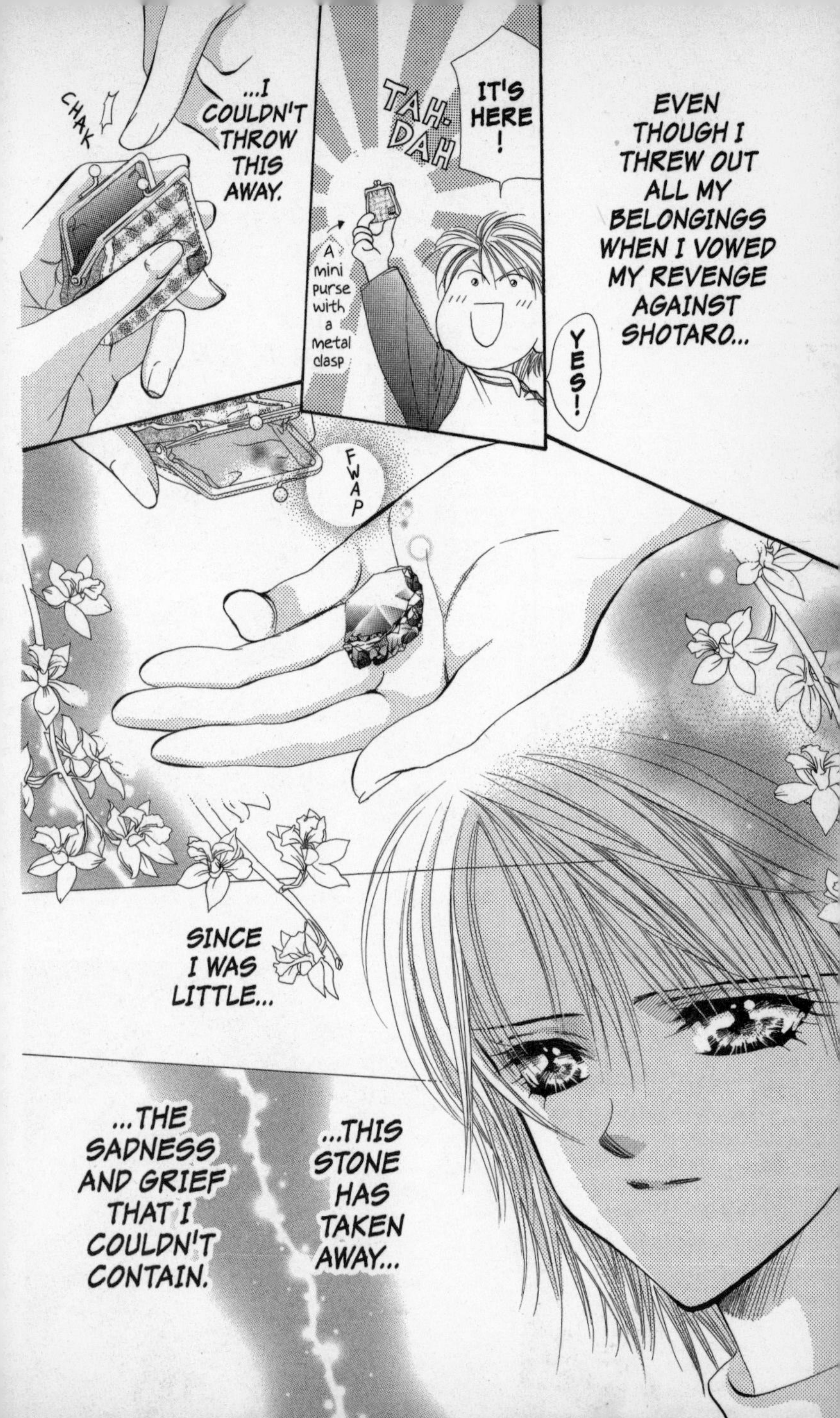
EVEN THOUGH I THREW OUT ALL MY BELONGINGS WHEN I VOWED MY REVENGE AGAINST SHOTARO...
IT'S HERE!
TAH-DAH
YES!
A mini purse with a metal clasp
...I COULDN'T THROW THIS AWAY.
CHAK
FWAP
SINCE I WAS LITTLE...
...THIS STONE HAS TAKEN AWAY...
...THE SADNESS AND GRIEF THAT I COULDN'T CONTAIN.

A MAGICAL STONE...

WELL...

...I MIGHT BELIEVE IT ONLY BECAUSE THAT'S WHAT I WAS TOLD WHEN I GOT IT...

That this stone eats sadness...

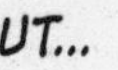

BUT...

See... already...

...My dark feelings, which were groveling deep underground...

...are about to come out of the ground, where the sky can be seen...

She IS the type to be easily duped.

...WHEN I HOLD IT IN MY HANDS, I FEEL BETTER...

IT MAY JUST BE ME...

...BUT...

...THIS STONE, WHICH SOOTHES ME EVEN NOW...

...USED TO BE...

...AND IS EVEN NOW...

...MY SECRET TREASURE.

WHEN I'M ABLE TO...

...LAUGH LIKE ALWAYS...

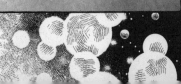

...I WILL THINK ABOUT WHAT TO DO FROM NOW ON.

BECAUSE...
I DON'T THINK...
HA HA!
...IT'S FOR ME!
...EVEN IF I DID MY BEST...
...I CAN'T PUT THINGS BACK TO-GETHER.
YES-TER-DAY...
...I REALIZED WHAT WAS WRONG WITH ME.
ONCE I SHAT-TERED INTO PIECES...
...EVEN IF YOU PUT THOSE PIECES BACK TOGETHER...
...THEY WON'T BECOME WHOLE...
YOU'RE GIVING UP?

I...
... BELIEVED YOU WERE SERIOUS.
THAT'S WHY I LENT YOU MY PRECIOUS TOOLS.

.....

TAISHO ...

I...

... THOUGHT ...

...YOU HAD MORE GUTS THAN THAT.

HUH?
UH...
LME Talent Agency
Really, President?
YES. ALTHOUGH I CROSSED HER OUT ONCE, I WAS HAVING SECOND THOUGHTS, WHICH IS RARE.
SO IT'S ALL RIGHT.
SHUFF SHUFF
WELL...I CONSULTED YOU BECAUSE I WAS WONDERING ABOUT HER.
But that was only yesterday, and you've already made up your mind today?!
WEEEELL, I WAS INTERESTED IN HER PECULIAR PERSONALITY.

IF WE TRAINED HER FROM SCRATCH...
...she may...
...TURN OUT TO BE A REAL BOMB!
It sounds fun, so do it.

PRESIDENT...
BUT...
Wait a minute.
...SHE DOES LACK AN IMPORTANT EMOTION.
THAT IS WHY...
...IF SHE COMES TO ME...

...IT MEANS SHE CAN'T GIVE UP...
THAT HER PASSION MAKES UP FOR THE MISSING EMOTION...
...AND THIS PLAN WILL BE SET IN MOTION.
....

SHE'LL BE ALL RIGHT!
THAT GIRL IS...
...A PICTURE OF PERSISTENCE AND GUTS!
YES.
Ugh, that's not very Beautiful.
Pres

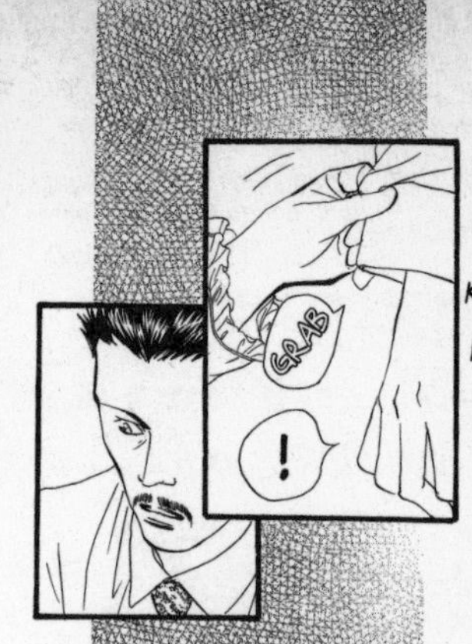
GRAB
!

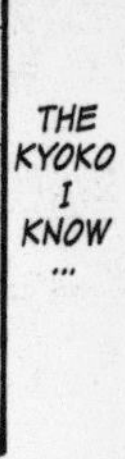
THE KYOKO I KNOW ...

... WON'T GIVE UP...
... AFTER JUST ONE FAILURE.

SHE WILL...
...COME BACK...

...TO LME!
HOMES UNDER

End of Act 5

Skip-Beat! End Notes

Everyone knows how to be a fan, but sometimes cool things from other cultures need a little help crossing the language barrier.

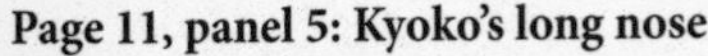

Page 11, panel 5: Kyoko's long nose

In Japanese, someone who's very boastful or vain is described as being a Tengu. A Tengu is a mountain spirit who has wings and a long nose.

Page 14, panel 3: The hand coming from Kyoko's throat

In Japanese, there's an expression "to want so much that a hand comes out of the throat." This is a visual representation of that expression.

Page 19, panel 5: The Taisho

In traditional Japanese restaurants, the master is called "Taisho" and his wife is called "Okami-san." The employees call them by their title, as do the customers.

Page 21, panel 7: Kyoko isn't going to high school

Compulsory education in Japan is only up to ninth grade, so Kyoko doesn't have to finish high school.

Page 30, panel 2: Inn proprietress

In Japanese inns, the "face" of the inn is the proprietress (okami-san), who greets guests and takes care of the customers. The husband stays in the background, taking care of management duties.

Page 33, panel 1: Kligo Pu★cchin Pudding

In Japan, there is a Glico product called Pucchin Purin. The "pucchin" describes popping a pin on the bottom on the container, which lets air in and makes the pudding drop out.

Page 59, panel 1: Kyoko's bow
This is a formal way to greet a person, called "Mitsuyubi", where three fingers of each hand rest on the tatami mat. Mitsuyubi literally means "three fingers."

Page 66, panel 4: The big sneeze
In Japan, sneezing is a sign that people are talking about you. Sneeze once and you are being praised, twice and you are being criticized, three times and you are being laughed at (or admired or scolded), and four times means you will catch a cold.

Page 70, panel 3: Talento
"Talentos", or talents in Japan usually appear on various TV shows as regulars, but they may also appear in dramas/movies/commercials, MC a show, sing and put out CDs, write magazine columns/essays/books, etc.

Page 93, panel 3: Oricon
Oricon is the Japanese equivalent of the Billboard Music Chart.

Page 101, panel 2: Straw doll
In Japan straw dolls can be used, much like voodoo dolls, to put a curse on someone.

Page 101, panel 3: Mo!
A Japanese exclamation similar to "geez."

Page 133, panel 3: Katsura-muki
A technique for peeling daikon radish (and other vegetables, like cucumber and carrot) into paper-thin strips, which then are used in food presentation and preparation.

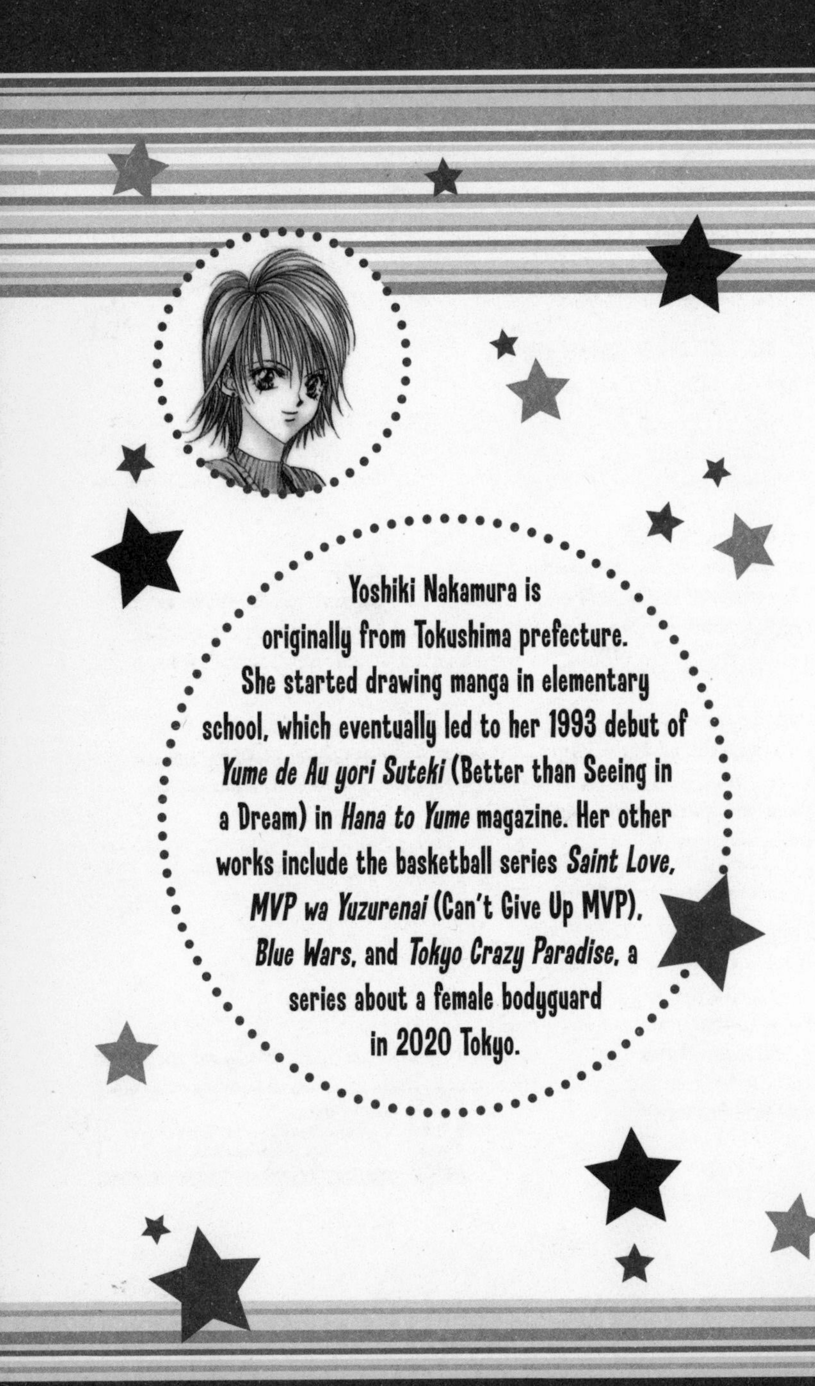

Yoshiki Nakamura is originally from Tokushima prefecture. She started drawing manga in elementary school, which eventually led to her 1993 debut of *Yume de Au yori Suteki* (Better than Seeing in a Dream) in *Hana to Yume* magazine. Her other works include the basketball series *Saint Love*, *MVP wa Yuzurenai* (Can't Give Up MVP), *Blue Wars*, and *Tokyo Crazy Paradise*, a series about a female bodyguard in 2020 Tokyo.

SKIP·BEAT!

Vol. 1

The Shojo Beat Manga Edition

STORY AND ART BY YOSHIKI NAKAMURA

English Translation & Adaptation/Tomo Kimura
Touch-up Art & Lettering/Sabrina Heep
Design/Yukiko Whitley
Editor/Pancha Diaz

Editor in Chief, Books/Alvin Lu
Editor in Chief, Magazines/Marc Weidenbaum
VP of Publishing Licensing/Rika Inouye
VP of Sales/Gonzalo Ferreyra
Sr. VP of Marketing/Liza Coppola
Publisher/Hyoe Narita

Printed in Canada

Published by VIZ Media, LLC
P.O. Box 77010
San Francisco, CA 94107

Shojo Beat Manga Edition
10 9 8 7 6 5 4 3
First printing, July 2006
Third printing, December 2007

RATED T FOR TEEN

PARENTAL ADVISORY
SKIP·BEAT! is rated T for Teen and is recommended for ages 13 and up. This volume contains suggestive themes.

ratings.viz.com

The gripping story — in manga format

Get the complete *Be With You* collection— buy the manga and fiction today!

www.viz.com

Shojo
Beat
MANGA from the HEART
THE REAL DRAMA BEGINS IN...

viz media

RATED T TEEN

RATED
T+
FOR OLDER TEEN
ratings.viz.com